LEATHERPORT, OHIO

LEATHERPORT, OHIO

STORIES FROM THE GREAT BLACK SWAMP

NYLE KARDATZKE

Editorial Services: Karen Roberts, RQuest, LLC

Cover: 1106 Design

Printed in the United States of America

For permission to use material, contact:
Nyle Kardatzke
Email: nylebk@gmail.com

ISBN: 978-1-7328222-2-1 (print)
        978-1-7328222-3-8 (eBook)

OTHER BOOKS BY NYLE KARDATZKE

Widow-man: A Widower's Story and Journaling Book, 2014

The Brown House Stories: A Child's Garden of Eden, 2015

The Clock of the Covenant, 2016

The Summertime of Our Lives: Stories from a Marriage, 2019

Dedication

Dedicated to those who drained the swamp and to their descendants, especially those of the Elmore Class of 1957 and the teachers who opened the world to them.

Contents

Contents

Preface

Winesburg, Ohio, by Sherwood Anderson is based loosely on the town of Clyde, Ohio, only twenty-four miles from Leatherport, Ohio. But while the Winesburg of Anderson's book is a fictional town based on the historic Clyde, there was an actual settlement called Leatherport. Its history was so brief as to make it nearly mythical.

Leatherport, Ohio, like Winesburg, Ohio, looks closely at the people and activities in a small area in Northwest Ohio. In both books, readers explore actual lives intertwined in a bygone way of life. Because of the similarities, this book could have the same subtitle as Sherwood Anderson's: A Group of Tales of Ohio Small Town Life. This book's subtitle, Tales from the Great Black Swamp, is a reminder of the deep, forbidding swamp and forest that delayed development of an area in Northwest Ohio. For me, growing up outside Elmore, a small town near Leatherport, the stories are personal.

As a teenager living in Clyde, Ohio, Sherwood Anderson worked at The Elmore Manufacturing Company assembling bicycles. The company was founded in Elmore in 1893, but it moved to Clyde in 1912, four years before publication of *Winesburg*. There is no evidence that Sherwood Anderson visited Elmore, but if he did, he surely would have seen the similarities between the two towns.

Leatherport sat on the high north bank of the Portage River with the Great Black Swamp just to its north. Water on the north side of the river flowed mostly to the north through the swamp in drowsy, slow-moving shallow streams barely deep enough to be called creeks. Across the Portage River, runoff from forests and farms flowed north into the river and made it large enough for small trading boats that reached this far inland from Lake Erie.

The tiny traders' settlement of Leatherport vanished soon after it was named in the mid-1800s. Leatherport's name has survived only in the minds of a few local people and in the name of the one-room Leatherport School that once stood to its north on Graytown Road.

The Great Black Swamp, drained long ago, lingers on in clumps of woods amid farm fields and orchards. Those lands are drained by ditches and by millions of field tiles lying just a few feet down beneath rich swamp soil.

Prologue

A MYSTICAL FEELING HOVERS OVER the countryside in Northwestern Ohio on cool September mornings. To the more imaginative minds, its flat farmlands studded with clumps of woods might suggest medieval castles.

This region of Ohio was once known as the Great Black Swamp, and its geologic past explains its appearance today. During the great glacial period that ended 14,000 years ago, a mile-high glacier pressed down on the earth and flattened the land, creating a swamp floor that was utterly flat. Shallow water covered most of the land nearly year-round and collected leaves that decayed year after year. Eventually the swamp was covered with trees so tall they blotted out the sun in the summer. Drowsy, shallow creeks meandered slowly through the swamp, connecting with three larger streams that led north to Lake Erie.

Insects, birds, and animals populated the swamp. Fallen trees and tangled underbrush made the area nearly impassable. A few trails led through the swamp along creeks or on slightly higher ridges left by the retreating glacier. Native Americans, the earliest explorers, once used the trails, but most trails wouldn't support the wagons and farm equipment of the later-arriving settlers. To cross through the swamp could take weeks for travelers, so it remained undeveloped until the 1850s. People migrating westward generally chose to pass either south of the swamp or to go around it by boat on Lake Erie.

If you have ever traveled across Northwestern Ohio on the Ohio Turnpike, you have driven through the land of the Black Swamp. You probably wouldn't have noticed remnants of the swamp, only the very level farmland and beautiful crops. You wouldn't have become mired in mud like the earliest travelers either. It's too late to experience the troubles and mysteries of the swamp.

The region once known as the Great Black Swamp was drained long ago for farming. It now produces tomatoes, cucumbers, sugar beets, peppers, and sweet corn. Its fertile farms and small towns are situated near Toledo. Only a few short stories of life in the early days have been captured in writings. This collection, *Leatherport, Ohio,* offers both historical information and whimsical tales about life in the Great Black Swamp from the earliest days of settlement to the mid-1900s.

The Forgotten Indians

Late in production of this book, an Elmore classmate suggested I mention the American Indians (or Native Americans) who had lived in Northern Ohio for centuries. His suggestion made me realize how remote the Indians had seemed to most Leatherport folk in the 1900s. We heard of ancient arrowheads being found on Portage River floodlands near Elmore, but little else was said of Indians. The Black Swamp area is sprinkled with Indian names such as Ottawa, Erie, Maumee, and Sandusky, but people in rural Leatherport were too preoccupied with draining and taming the swamp to pause over the area's more ancient history. We kids played "cowboys and Indians" at recess time, but our imaginary world was always far to the west, never in Ohio. And our focus was always on the cowboys, not the Indians.

(A quick online search will provide detailed information about Ohio's early Indians.)

The Great Black Swamp

The Great Black Swamp once extended from Fort Wayne, Indiana, to Toledo, Ohio, along both sides of the Maumee River. On the east side of the river, it stretched for fifty miles.

The swamp was called "black" because it was like a jungle, in constant shade in the warm months. Gigantic trees stretched up a hundred feet, and a canopy of vines kept the swamp's standing water in darkness, even at mid-day. The blackness of the swamp was mirrored in its ponds of stagnant water and rotted leaves.

The Great Black Swamp supported wildlife: muskrats, raccoons, opossums, snakes, turtles, and cranes. The swamp was home to clouds of mosquitoes that swarmed over early settlers. The mosquitoes carried malarial fever and caused aching muscles the settlers called "ague." Living in the area was not safe or healthy in the early days.

To envision swamp life in the 1840s, think of a small log house surrounded by tall trees. Smoke curls from a plastered log chimney. A fire smolders near the door to repel mosquitoes. Life in such cabins was crude. Only essential tools, clothing, bedding, storage containers, and food were on hand. Now imagine this little cabin alone, with no others in sight.

The long process of draining the Great Black Swamp began in the 1820s, when European settlers first penetrated the area. In those early days, "draining the swamp" was not a metaphor or a political slogan. It was the real thing in a real swamp filled with real water, bugs, reptiles, and diseases.

Drainage began with hand-dug, shallow ditches near existing, nearly stagnant streams. Over time the ditches and streams were deepened and widened. One stream was named the La Carpe Creek in honor of carp, those lazy, bottom-feeding fish that live in slow-moving Ohio streams. It was widened as it flowed east across Graytown Road to a north–south swale a half mile farther east. In the 1940s, the swale was widened and deepened to create a much larger ditch that flows straight south, through farm fields, to the Portage River.

In the 1860s, a small factory began making field tiles and red clay bricks on Graytown Road, a half mile north of the Portage River. This was the Gleckler Tile Yard. Drainage tiles from this factory and others were laid under farm fields, and ground water flowed to roadside ditches. Swamp land began to produce corn and beans instead of snakes and mosquitoes.

My father, Arlin Kardatzke, inherited the "swamp-draining gene" from his grandfather, Christopher Gleckler, the founder of the tile and brick factory, the Gleckler Tile Yard. As a hobby in his later years, Arlin studied maps of the area and the early farmers' problems in diverting water off their land. He could see from topographical maps that the land was almost perfectly flat, with some areas having only an inch of elevation change in a mile.

In the spirit of swamp drainage, Arlin made 30-inch concrete tiles and placed them in the deep ditch along his property on Graytown Road. To make his tiles, Arlin borrowed two cylindrical steel forms. The smaller cylinder fit inside the larger one with a 2-inch gap all the way around. He rented an electric-powered cement mixer that he filled again and again with sand, gravel, and cement. He poured wet cement into the gap between the forms and let it dry a few days before lifting the forms off each new tile. He repeated this process dozens of times until he had enough tiles to line the bottom of the ditch for about a hundred yards in front of his property.

It was staggeringly hard work for Arlin, but he found joy in beautifying his part of the Great Black Swamp. His homemade tiles now lie under lawns along the road in front of the pond properties.

Leatherport, Ohio

If you look up "Leatherport" on Google Maps, you won't find it in Ohio or anywhere else. It was a tiny settlement on the north side of the Portage River that flourished briefly and soon disappeared. The name of the place has survived mainly in the vocabularies of a few people who heard of Leatherport in their childhood nearly a century ago.

The geographical heart of Leatherport lies buried in a few concrete foundations, covered long ago by tall grass, on the north bank of the Portage River at the south end of Graytown Road. The economic and religious capital of Leatherport was in Elmore, two miles to its southwest, but its intellectual capital until 1925 was the Leatherport School.

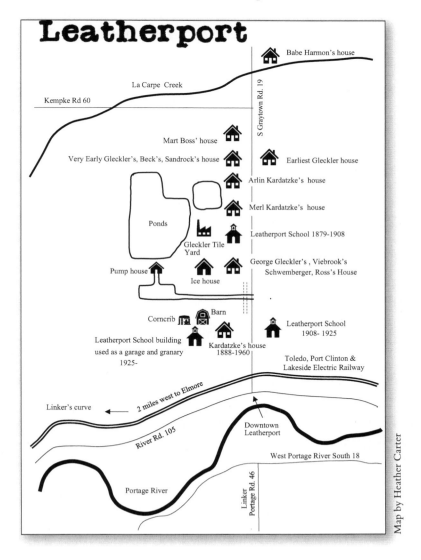

Leatherport

- Babe Harmon's house
- La Carpe Creek
- Kempke Rd 60
- S Graytown Rd. 19
- Mart Boss' house
- Very Early Gleckler's, Beck's, Sandrock's house
- Earliest Gleckler house
- Arlin Kardatzke's house
- Merl Kardatzke's house
- Ponds
- Gleckler Tile Yard
- Leatherport School 1879-1908
- Pump house
- Ice house
- George Gleckler's, Viebrook's Schwemberger, Ross's House
- Corncrib
- Barn
- Leatherport School building used as a garage and granary 1925-
- Kardatzke's house 1888-1960
- Leatherport School 1908- 1925
- Toledo, Port Clinton & Lakeside Electric Railway
- Linker's curve
- 2 miles west to Elmore
- River Rd. 105
- Downtown Leatherport
- West Portage River South 18
- Portage River
- Linker Portage Rd. 46

Map by Heather Carter

The Leatherport School

The one-room building known simply as the Leatherport School, when it was new, stood a half mile north of "downtown Leatherport" on the west side of Graytown Road, next to the pond that's still there. It was built on a half-acre of land that my great-grandfather Christopher Gleckler loaned to Harris Township in 1879 for use as a schoolyard and only as a school-yard. Christopher already operated the tile and brick factory next to the new schoolyard, and he soon built a house beside the school and factory. His son, George Gleckler, took over the factory when Christopher died.

Kids from farms within a mile or two attended the Leatherport School. My grandparents, Fred Kardatzke and Emma Gleckler, lived on Graytown Road near the school and were schooled there in the 1890s. My grand-mother told us kids that the maple trees in the old schoolyard were already big when she started school there in 1889. Now, more than a hundred years later, some of those giant old maple trees are still standing.

The Gleckler Tile Factory stood immediately to the west of the Leatherport School at the turn of the twentieth century. Clouds of black smoke from the tile factory's coal-fired kilns blew through the schoolyard and through the

The tile yard smoke that moved the Leatherport School.

school's open windows. As a young mother, Emma was worried that smoke from her brother's factory would be unhealthy for her children when they were old enough to go to school. She insisted that the building be moved away from the smoke before her first child, Harris, was old enough to start school.

In 1908, at Emma's insistence, the schoolhouse was jacked up, placed on logs, rolled a quarter mile south down Graytown Road, and placed in a field on the east side of the road opposite the family home. No smoke from the tile yard would clog the lungs of schoolchildren there. My father and his eight siblings began their schooling in the same one-room schoolhouse in which their parents Fred and Emma had studied many years earlier.

Leatherport School students in about 1894 at the school's original site downwind from the Gleckler Tile Yard. A surly Fred Kardatzke is in the back row. His future bride is in front in a plaid dress.

Leatherport, Ohio

(In the extremely dry summer of 1982, the grass dried unevenly above the foundation at the school's 1879–1908 location. The driest grass showed that the school was 36 feet long from east to west, and 24 feet wide from north to south. The school's southeast corner was 10 feet north of the hand pump that still stands where it pumped water for the school's young students and their teachers so long ago.)

The school's new location was closer to the old Leatherport settlement, so its name added new life to the name. School consolidation eventually doomed the Leatherport School as it did most other one-room schools in Ohio in the early 1900s. The Leatherport School was closed in 1925, and kids were bused to a new school in Elmore.

After the school closed, my grandfather Fred Kardatzke bought the building and moved it again, this time across Graytown Road to his house on the west side of the road. Wooden rollers were placed under it a second time so that it could be rolled straight west across the field and lawn. A sunporch and laundry room on the west side of the house had to be torn down so the school could pass narrowly by the main portion of the house. From there it was rolled straight north, just missing the main kitchen. The demolished rooms were rebuilt and remain on the west side of the house.

The school building was placed on a concrete foundation, and Fred Kardatzke used it as a garage and grain bin. Paintings of pastoral scenes still adorned the walls from the building's schoolhouse days, and the scent of wheat piled high there evoked something powerful in his grandchildren. Mice and small kids alike enjoyed the perfume of golden wheat stored there. In the 1940s and 1950s the floor creaked underfoot and groaned when my grandfather parked his big black Buick inside.

In the 1990s, 110 years after the school was built, a new owner of the property demolished the old school building because it was no longer safe for cars or people. You can imagine it as it once was if you look at the white garage at the farmhouse less than half a mile north of Route 105 on Graytown Road.

(In 1949 there was a reunion of former Leatherport School students at the old school on the Fred Kardatzke property. Fred had died in March that year, and this was the last reunion in the former school building. The elderly people at the reunion

Leatherport School Reunion, July 1949.

were even older than the people at our church. I was a renegade nine-year old and delighted in swilling down carbonated "pop." Other kids circulated a rumor that one of the old ladies had gargled with the pink lemonade and had spat it back into the punch bowl. We all opted for factory-bottled "pop.")

Graytown, Ohio

Graytown is about three miles north of what might be called "downtown Leatherport." It formed as a railroad depot town when the first railroad penetrated the Great Black Swamp. It's an unincorporated community of perhaps two hundred people now, home to a post office, a grain elevator and other farm businesses, and a pizza restaurant, the Country Keg. Its elementary school closed in 2012 after a lively history in three buildings, beginning with a log cabin.

In Leatherport's early days, Graytown roared and rumbled under the weight of several trains each day and night on the New York Central line.

Besides freight, passenger trains zoomed through, including the Twentieth Century Limited. Graytown, over the years, has been home to a sawmill, a blacksmith shop, a cider press business, a hotel, and at least one saloon. One saloon is said to have perished during Prohibition. At a clover-drying factory in town, clover blossoms picked by local families once were dried for reasons unknown to anyone in Graytown today.

Elmore, Ohio

Although few living today have heard of Leatherport, many have heard of the town of Elmore, situated two miles southwest, upriver on the Portage River. Elmore's earliest settlers came in the 1820s, and the town won the race to become the commercial center of what became Harris Township. By the end of the 1800s, it was home to a Catholic church and several protestant churches.

In the early 1800s, before the Great Black Swamp was drained, Elmore's greatest natural resource was an exposed slab of natural limestone in the river. The flat limestone attracted Native Americans as an easy place to portage their canoes from one patch of smooth water to another. Europeans later found the limestone a good place to ford the river in low water on foot or with heavy wagons. The same limestone in the Portage River supports the new highway bridge if you enter Elmore heading south from Toledo.

Elmore is located in Harris Township, one of the twelve townships of Ottawa County, Ohio. More than half of the population of Harris Township is in Elmore. The town's current population of 1,410 is about the same as it was shortly after the Civil War, but the names of the people have changed even though their number has remained the same.

"Downtown Leatherport"

The three men who gave Leatherport its name probably would laugh to hear talk of a downtown in their little settlement. When they endowed the area with the name "Leatherport," there were only three small businesses on a muddy road above the river. A few crude farm buildings and some trappers' cabins were scattered in the forest to the north. But the spirit of

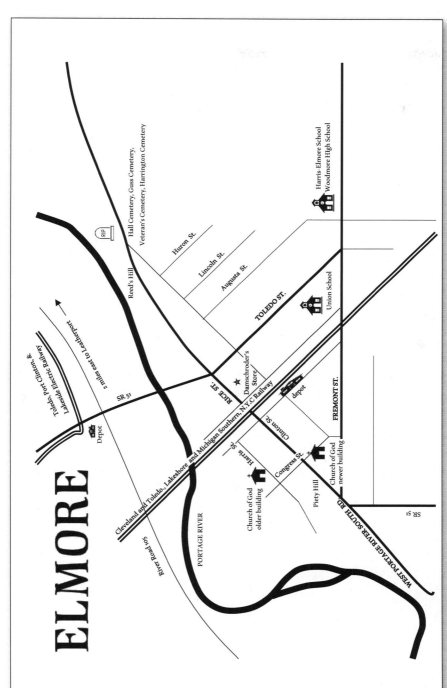

ELMORE

Map by Heather Carter

commerce was upon the three shopkeepers, and they felt their settlement should have a name. Since the leather tanner had been there first, they decided to name the place "Leatherport." The "port" portion of the settlement's name referred to its location at one of the farthest points where boats from Lake Erie could travel inland to pick up or deposit cargo.

Author Newell Witte reports the naming this way:

> Nicholas Wallace purchased a few acres of land along the river near the Graytown Road in 1834. Here he erected a tannery. Nearby Robert Morse built the first blacksmith shop in the area and John Yost, a cobbler, erected a place of business. With a blacksmith shop, shoe shop, and tannery, the settlers thought they should form a village, so Joseph Wardlow named the place "Leatherport" in honor of Mr. Wallace, the tanner. (*Elmore's 100 Years, 1851–1951,* Witte, 1951, p. 21)

Leatherport's days were numbered by the growth of Elmore, two miles farther upstream. The exposed limestone bedrock blocked further boat travel except by portaging canoes around the shallows, but it was a perfect place for a railroad bridge over the Portage River. In 1852, a railroad bridge was built in the growing town of Elmore, making it the hub of local commerce. That railroad bridge was one of a succession of bridges over the Portage River. When Elmore grew as a railroad town, Leatherport dwindled away, never becoming large enough to be called a town. Eventually no businesses and only a few houses were left.

The crumbling concrete foundation of a building is all you will find of downtown Leatherport today, and even spotting that will take some luck in the tall grass. The stories that follow offer glimpses of historic Leatherport and the lives of those who lived there and in the nearby settlements.

(Detailed maps of Leatherport, historic Elmore, one-room schools, and Portage River bridges have been drawn by Heather Carter of Elmore. Some of the maps are available at the Elmore General Store.)

Part One

Tales from the
Great Black Swamp

1
Dynamiting Fish

WHEN THE BLACK SWAMP LAND WAS being cleared for farming, dynamite was a friend of farmers around Leatherport. They usually kept dynamite in the corncrib or another small farm building, not in the big barn and for sure not in the house.

Farmers routinely used dynamite to blast big stumps out of the ground to clear fields for corn or beans or wheat or oats. To prepare for the blast, an auger on the end of a five-foot steel rod was twisted into the ground under a stump, cutting roots as well as dirt. The auger and rod made a hole about three inches in diameter, where sticks of dynamite could be slipped in under the stump. A fuse was then extended to a blasting cap, which would set off the dynamite and blast the stump out of the ground. Once out of the ground, the big, gnarly stump was burned so the land could be cleared for plowing and planting. In the 1940s, when I was a boy, we could sometimes hear the low, dull "whoomp" of a 1,000-pound stump being blasted out of the ground.

In 1893, my Grampa Fred Kardatzke was a ten-year old boy, too young for the heaviest farm work but old enough for mischief and adventures. He knew about dynamite's uses on the farm. Like many ten-year old boys, my Grampa Fred probably felt in his bones that nothing very bad could happen to him. But if things had gone differently on one particular day, my father and I would not have been born because my grandfather would have been blown to bits.

It was probably a drowsy summer day, when farm work had been slow for a few days, and the "dog days of summer" hung heavy on young boys around Leatherport. During those July and August days, the weather was usually hot and sultry, and boys sometimes gazed at clouds and thought of flying like birds. Fishing would be fun, but it meant digging worms, a hot chore, and fish were sometimes too sleepy to bite worms. Thoughts of fishing led two boys to think of the most exciting way they knew to catch fish: blasting them right out of the river.

Even as a young boy, Fred knew about blasting fish. Here's how it worked: Somebody would light the fuse on a 12-inch red stick of dynamite, throw the dynamite as far as possible out onto the river, and watch for it to go off. Boom! It would explode and send up a geyser of water. As the water settled back into the river, fish floated to the top. Some were dead. Some were only stunned and would soon swim away. The larger fish were the most fun. The people doing the blasting could wade into the water and pick up as many as they wanted for dinner.

One hot summer day, Fred went to the kitchen when no one was there and pocketed some big wooden kitchen matches. He went to the corncrib to the basket of dynamite. He looked around to see if anyone was watching and slipped three sticks of dynamite into a gunnysack. To make sure his actions looked like a regular fishing trip, he got his cane pole from the barn, but he never intended to use it that day. Just then his neighbor Will Gleckler walked into the yard.

"Ready to do some fishing?" Fred asked.

"What's the bag for?"

"Whad'ya think?"

Fred opened the bag for Will to see.

"Wow! Three of 'em! Think your dad will notice?"

"Don't think so. There are lots more in there. Let's get going."

It was less than half a mile down Graytown Road from Fred's house to the Portage River. The road ended at a bluff above the river. The River Road ran along that bluff from Elmore on east to Oak Harbor. The boys took a well-worn wagon trail that in earlier times had led to Harrison's Crossing. Following the rutted track down the steep slope to the riverbank, Fred was careful not to let the bag of dynamite bang hard against any trees or rocks, thinking it might explode.

The Portage River was low at that time of summer, so the water took its lazy time on the way to Lake Erie. On any other summer day, the boys would have baited their hooks with worms and waited to see what under-water creature would grab them. Worms were great bait, but dynamite was quicker, surer, and more exciting—and the noise it made was wonderful.

The riverbank was silent where they sat except for buzzing insects and a few birds calling. River Road above them was silent too. It was noon, and most farmers were at home having their "dinner," which was what most people now call "lunch." Later in the day, families would gather for the last meal of the day, what they called "supper."

Fred looked around at Will. "Ready for some fun?"

"Yep! You want to throw the first one?" Will replied.

"Okay," Fred told him. "I'll hold it, and you light it. I'll throw it out to the middle."

Fred took a stick of dynamite from the bag and laid the bag down on the bank. He gave Will two matches, and they went to the river's edge.

"Okay, light'er up!" Fred said.

Will struck one of the matches on a rock, and Fred reached over toward the flame with the tip of the dynamite. He held the fuse in the flame until it fumed and sprayed sparks angrily. He let the fuse burn a few seconds, cocked his arm and threw the dynamite high and far out into the river.

The fuse kept sputtering in the water for a few seconds, and then, Boom! The dynamite went off with terrific force. A beautiful white tower of water shot up from the river and then fell back down like rain.

When the last drops of water had settled, catfish, rock bass, bluegills, a gar, and several hefty carp bobbed to the surface and floated on their sides. The boys especially liked seeing the carp because they were the biggest. One was over a foot long.

"You done good, Fred!" Will yelled. "Look at all them fish! My turn now!"

Will took a stick of dynamite from the bag and came back to Fred.

"Think you can throw it as far as I did?" Fred asked.

"I hope so. I hope I can get it far enough from us before it goes off," Will replied.

"You better," Fred warned. "We don't want our folks finding us floating down the river."

Will held out his dynamite, and Fred lit it. The fuse sputtered and smoked and sparkled like before. Will threw the dynamite almost as far as Fred had thrown his. Again, river water leapt up in a beautiful plume, high above the river, and settled down again. More fish came to the top, and there was another big carp, bigger than any fish Fred's blast had brought to the top.

"Wow! That was a good one!" Will yelled.

"We got one more stick," Fred announced. "I better do it, since it's my dynamite."

Will didn't argue. After all, it *was* Fred's dad's dynamite.

Fred got the last stick of dynamite from the bag. Will struck the match, and Fred held the fuse in the flame. Like before, he let it burn a little to make sure it was burning.

Suddenly a rumbling sound came from the gravel up on River Road. A heavy farm wagon was going along the road. Fred was afraid it was his father. His father didn't like fun and didn't like fish, and he wouldn't think blasting fish should be fun. Without thinking, Fred hid the lit stick of dynamite behind his back. He felt something burning his hand. Sparks from the dynamite fuse bit his hand like mosquitoes. The fuse was still burning!

Fred whirled around and threw the dynamite out over the river. Boom! It went off in midair. Echoes ran up and down the river, louder than he and Will had ever heard. But the farm wagon above them on the road kept creaking and rumbling on. The driver didn't stop.

The boys looked at each other. "You coulda got blown up!" Will yelled.

"Yeah, but I didn't," Fred answered, "but it was close."

"Do you think the wagon man heard it?" Will asked.

"He mighta heard it, and he might not'a. The wagon was loud. He mighta thought somebody was blasting a stump," Fred answered. "Or maybe he just thought somebody might be down here blasting fish."

"If he thought that, he was right!" Will said.

That day may or may not have been the last time Fred blasted fish in the Portage River. Blasting fish was a popular sport until it was outlawed and dynamite disappeared from farms, so he may have risked his life again. Nothing was quite as exciting and noisy for a kid on a dog day of summer as dynamiting fish, especially if you nearly got killed.

2
The Bachelor and His Dogs

A RLIN K ARDATZKE, MY FATHER, once told me of a bachelor with a large collection of dogs who lived at the south end of Graytown Road. He may have had twenty dogs. He lived alone, and the dogs were like a family to him. He fed them as well as he could, and he talked to them morning and evening and any other time he might be in the house. He told them about his work in the fields and about his hunting trips. If something made him mad, the dogs were the first to hear about it. If he shot a rabbit or a pheasant, he gave the guts and skin to his dogs, and they considered it a beautiful treat.

The bachelor must have seemed like an odd duck to the local farm boys. They saw his funny clothing, his sagging old horse, and the swarm of dogs that slept in the house with him. Whenever he went to Elmore or

Elmore in early days with buggies like the bachelor's.

Graytown, he drove a lightweight buggy pulled by his decrepit old horse. The buggy was called a one-horse chaise (pronounced *shaze*), and it seemed odd after cars and the interurban train came to Leatherport.

The nearby farm boys could not leave this bit of living history alone. Several of them decided to dream up a prank to pull on the bachelor. The prank they decided on was to put his buggy on top of the little barn where he kept it, and they pulled their stunt one night near Halloween. How the boys got the buggy on the roof remained their secret for life, even when they became older, respectable farmers.

The roof was low enough that two or three of them could have climbed up on it while the others hoisted the buggy up to them. The boys on the ground might have attached a rope to the buggy and may have thrown the rope over the roof to use to pull the buggy up to the peak. They worked so silently that the bachelor and his dogs slept right through the crime. When they were finished, they left the buggy where it was perched, straddling the peak of the barn with two wheels on each slope. The boys disappeared into the night, restraining themselves from rolling on the grass laughing until they were far away from the bachelor's house.

The next morning, the bachelor blinked and gasped when he saw his buggy on top of the barn. He was furious. He grabbed his gun and marched around the barn to see if the culprits were still there in broad daylight. He grumbled and raged angrily all day.

That night as the bachelor filled the feeding pan for his dogs, he lectured them about their laziness. They hadn't barked while the buggy was being put on the barn roof. They should have barked. He kept his gun in his hands while he talked and the dogs ate. His sermon to his dogs went on and on, rising to a fevered pitch.

"If those boys ever come here again, I expect you to *bark!*" he yelled and jerked back, pulling the trigger. Blam! He shot a hole in the middle of the dogs' feeding pan. The dogs went howling away in all directions.

My father never told me what happened next. He never told me how he knew so many details about the bachelor and his dogs either. But he told the story so well that I didn't feel the need to ask for more.

3
The Calfy Pail

"Why is Ted running up the yard?" Ma asked. "Better check, Arlin."

Sure enough, Arlin Kardatzke's cousin Ted was running right up to the house. Arlin sprang to the door.

"They're draining the pond!" Ted nearly yelled. "The ditch is running like a river!"

Arlin looked to Ma. "Can I go see? I already shelled the corn for the chickens."

"Pa give you any other chores?" she asked him. Arlin shook his head.

"Okay. But you boys don't go a gittin' drownded! We don't need none of that!"

The two boys ran across the yard and onto the road before anyone could call for them to help with something. They didn't want anything to spoil this great time for play. The sun had come out and was warming the dry grass along the ditch bank beside the road. The air was cool, but in the warm sun they could feel summer coming with all the good things like going barefoot and catching frogs and freezing ice cream.

Deep water was flowing in the ditch from the tile-yard pond a half mile up the road. The boys knew that the land there was perfectly flat, so a flood of water in the ditch wasn't natural. It was man-made. George Gleckler was pumping water from the pond so he could restart the tile yard for another season of digging clay and making field tiles and bricks.

The pump house was pitching pond water over a dike, creating an artificial torrent of pond water that pushed down the ditch, past the barn, under the driveway, past the lawn and the house, and into the open mouth of a large tile that carried it down under the fields for a quarter of a mile to the Portage River. The open mouth of the tile was scary, even when the ditch was not flooded. To Arlin, it was like the open mouth of a monster or a serpent that wanted to swallow anyone who came too near.

The boys watched for a few minutes as the water rushed dangerously past them toward the mouth of the tile, but they were too excited to think about danger. Instead, they thought it would be an adventure to play along the ditch while the water was flowing through their flat farm country like a rushing mountain river.

"I have an idea!" Arlin said. He was looking into the ditch and the dark, swirling water.

Ted looked into the ditch, too, but he didn't have an idea. "What?" he asked.

"Let's play boats!" Arlin yelled.

Ted looked at the ditch again and remembered a boy in their class who had drowned while playing in a creek near town. The ditch wasn't as big as that creek, but there was probably enough water to drown an eight-year-old boy. Besides, the water was cold and muddy, and he especially didn't want to drown in water as cold and muddy as that.

"I ain't goin' in no boat in no muddy ditch today!" Ted replied.

"No! Not real boats! Play boats!" Arlin said. "Let's find boats to float down the ditch!"

Ted couldn't think of any boats they had. Arlin was a little older, so he could sometimes think of things sooner.

"Where we goin' to get boats?" Ted asked cautiously.

"Let's go look in the barn," Arlin suggested. "There's gotta be something there we can float down the ditch."

The boys trudged over to the red barn at Arlin's house, right next to the ditch. It seemed almost sure there would be at least one piece of something in the big barn that would make a fine boat, maybe more than one.

Just inside the door, there it was. It wasn't exactly a boat, but it would be fun to float it in the ditch. Both boys saw it at once, and Arlin said, "Yes, sir, there's our boat!"

"Yeah!" Ted yelled, but then he fell silent with a sad, dark thought. "Isn't that the calfy pail?" he asked softly.

"Sure, it's the calfy pail, but so what?" Arlin said, taking it from its hook on the wall.

"I thought you were never supposed to play with the calfy pail," Ted replied, almost whispering now. "I heard your pa say you could play with almost anything around the barn, but you should never touch the calfy pail."

Arlin knew Ted was right. He thought for a minute about what Pa had said, and he looked at the calfy pail again. The pail was special because it had a rubber nipple coming out its side at the bottom. The pail was used as a baby bottle for feeding milk to young calves that needed more milk than their own mother cows could provide. Arlin knew they would need the calfy pail at milking time, but that was a long way off. Besides, he was bigger now than when Pa had said not to play with it.

"Pa told me that when I was little. I think I can be careful enough now," Arlin said, taking care to leave the barn through the back door where they couldn't be seen from the house.

Arlin and Ted decided that one of them would take the pail upstream some distance and float it down to the other boy. That boy would grab it from the fast-moving ditch water. They would trade places, and the second boy would sail the pail down the flooded ditch.

Arlin took the first turn, running up the ditch a good long way. He carefully set the pail in the water and let it float down to Ted. Ted stepped down the steep ditch bank, reached out, and grabbed the handle. Then he ran upstream while Arlin ran downstream to catch the floating pail when Ted put it in. Again and again they ran along the road trading places, floating the calfy pail down the ditch.

After an hour, both boys were tired. They agreed to have just one more turn. This time, Arlin took the calfy pail an especially long way up the ditch. He waved to Ted that he was about to launch the boat, and Ted waved back. Arlin set the pail in the ditch, and it began bobbing down toward Ted as before.

Arlin sat down on the ditch bank to watch and rest. *It will have a long trip this time!* he thought.

At the other end, Ted saw that it would be awhile before the pail reached him, so he sat down on the ditch bank too. He looked at the white, fluffy clouds and thought about flying in a hot air balloon. From up there he would be able to see the calfy pail floating down the ditch.

Suddenly Ted remembered. "The calfy pail!"

He jumped up just in time to see it bobbing past him toward the barn.

Arlin had already seen the disaster from up the road. "The calfy pail! The calfy pail! Ted! Ted! Get the calfy pail!" he yelled as he ran.

Ted ran as fast as he could, but the pail was still ahead of him. He was gaining on it when it floated under the driveway bridge, and he was near it when it came out the other side in front of the lawn.

Ted slid down near the ditch, holding onto a clump of grass to avoid falling in. He was just even with the pail, and he grabbed for it. Just then the current pushed the pail to the other side of the ditch, and it floated on toward the mouth of the big drain tile. Both boys ran madly to catch up, but it was no use. The calfy pail was swallowed up by the big tile that led to the river.

"It's gone! It's gone!" Ted yelled and started to cry. "We lost the calfy pail!"

Arlin was furious. He heard himself yelling, "Ted! Ted! You old spitter! You old brat!" He didn't know where those words came from, especially "spitter." His mind must have made up that awful word just for this emergency.

Arlin wasn't crying yet, but he thought that this mistake was probably about the worst thing that had ever happened. What would happen to the calfies? What would happen to *him?* He pushed from his mind his father's stern warnings about playing with the calfy pail. He had to think fast.

"The river!" he yelled. "We'll catch it at the river! Run to the river!"

Arlin was off and running down the road before Ted saw through his tears where Arlin was going. Ted choked off his crying and did his best to keep up.

Down near the river, the drainage tile crossed under the road past where an ancient cider mill had been. It passed through a short canyon, crossed under River Road, and emptied into the Portage River. The calfy pail would have to come out there. The boys crossed the River Road and climbed down beside the rushing water as it plunged toward the river. There was just enough room to stand beside the mouth of the vaulted outlet without being swept into the even more dangerous water in the river.

If he had a long stick, Arlin reasoned, he might be able to fish out the calfy pail as it came floating by. With one hand, he held onto a sturdy little tree. He waited with a long stick in the other hand, hoping to snag the pail.

"Did you catch the calfy pail?" Ted yelled when he arrived.

"Not yet. I'm waiting for it," Arlin said.

"Can you catch it with that stick?" Ted wanted to know.

"I hope so," Arlin said with a sinking feeling. What if he couldn't and it got past them? What if the calfy pail didn't come out at all? What if it was already gone? He didn't want to think those awful thoughts.

The boys waited and waited for the calfy pail to come out. Arlin had to climb up on the bank and rest his arms a couple of times, always ready to lunge back toward the water to catch the calfy pail if it came. Finally it was time to give up. The calfy pail was a goner.

The two boys walked wearily and fearfully toward home. At Arlin's house they parted, and Ted started for his house, back up the road. They both knew not to tell anyone. What they had done was such a bad thing that they didn't want anyone to know. What would Pa say? What would he do? Arlin tried not to think about the razor strap his father kept behind the pantry door.

"Are you and Ted alright?" his mother asked as Arlin stepped almost silently into the mud porch and slipped off his boots.

"Yup," he said as calmly as possible.

"You lost the calfy pail, din' ya?"

His heart slammed hard against his chest and then seemed to stop. *She knows! This is it! This is the end!* he thought. *The calfy pail really is gone, and Ma knows who lost it and how.*

"How did you know?" Arlin blurted out, nearly crying.

"I seen you and Ted with it down by the ditch, and you scared me half a death yelling your way to the river. Ain't nobody in Leatherport dint hear about the calfy pail before it hit the river," his Ma replied matter-of-factly, still stirring something at the stove.

Arlin stared at the other side of the kitchen, thinking to himself. *If only I hadn't yelled. Why wasn't I quiet? Why did Ted have to cry?*

"I'll tell your Pa how you tried to catch it ennaway," Ma said reassuringly.

That was his only hope. He did try to catch the calfy pail, even when it was dangerous. He had been brave. Maybe Pa would take pity on him.

That night Arlin was in the corncrib shelling corn for the chickens when his father came home. Arlin decided this would be a good time to shell some extra corn. Pa went in the house, but Arlin didn't hear sounds of angry talking. That might be a good sign. Finally, Ma called everyone to supper.

The other children were already inside when Arlin reached the house. He could hear laughing inside, and he wondered if he would ever be able to laugh again. The laughing stopped when he entered the mud porch. He kicked off his boots and stepped through the kitchen doorway. Pa had just finished washing his hands.

"I hear you lost the calfy pail," Pa said, sounding very much to Arlin like the Lord when he found the children of Israel sinning.

Everyone looked at Arlin, and Pa looked right at him, too.

"I guess you'll have to get the calfy a new pail," he said after a pause. "Got any money?"

Arlin looked at Pa and said nothing. Pa didn't say anything more about the calfy pail. He must have been very tired that night. He walked slowly to his place at the table, looking over the steaming food.

"Let's eat," Pa said, and everyone passed the food.

It was a good supper that night, and it was better the next night when no one mentioned the calfy pail all day. Arlin gave Ma the money he had been saving for a toy airplane, and Pa bought a new calfy pail at the grain elevator.

Before long, the three calfies were so big they didn't need the new calfy pail anymore, but Arlin never, ever touched the calfy pail again.

Where the calfy pail was last seen.

4
The Legacy of the Calfy Pail

ARLIN AND TED MADE FREQUENT TRIPS to the river that year to see if the calfy pail ever came out and got caught on a tree or a root or a rock at the end of the big drain tile. They looked for many weeks, but it never appeared. In the summer, when the ditch was dry, they crawled down the drain tile a short way from its mouth to see if they could find it there, but they had no luck. They didn't crawl all the way to the river, knowing that was too dangerous. Snakes or other animals might be hiding in the tile. They also crawled up the tile from the river, but the calfy pail wasn't there either.

Both boys forgot about the calfy pail until Arlin told the story to his children many years later. When *those* children grew up, they told the story to *their* children. All the children and their children eventually made the trip back to Leatherport, and they all went to the river several times to look for the calfy pail.

As far as I know, no one ever found the calfy pail; but even today, whenever Arlin's grandkids or great-grandkids visit the property on Graytown Road, they ask each other, "Do you think the calfy pail is still stuck in the drain tile?" Everybody laughs.

(This story made me want to remember some of the things that happened to me when I was a boy so I would have stories to tell my children. And now you can tell the calfy pail story.)

5
"Pop! Goes the Weasel"

EMMA KARDATZKE WENT TO THE chicken coop to gather the eggs on a beautiful, warm fall day. She was thinking about what a good farm she and Fred had and about the work she had planned for the day. The little red chicken coop with its white trim and sloping roof looked happy and prosperous, a cozy home for her laying hens.

When she reached the chicken coop, something was wrong. White feathers were on the grass outside the coop, and some of them were splattered with bright red blood. Emma flung open the door. She looked in and screamed. There on the straw and chicken droppings were two dead hens.

The varmint that had gotten into the coop overnight and killed them was long gone, and she couldn't even see how it could have gotten inside. The way the chickens were killed looked to her like the work of a weasel, and Emma was shocked and angry. They were good, innocent chickens, and she couldn't afford to lose them. She choked back tears and carefully gathered the morning's eggs.

As she walked back to the house, Emma plotted how she would find and stop the murderous weasel, but when she got into the house, other things had to be done. She couldn't spend any more time that day thinking about a useless search for the weasel. Fred would have to take on the weasel problem when he came in from the fields.

Emma told Fred about the dead hens when he came in to clean up for dinner at noon. "Two more dead chickens," she said. "Blood all over 'em, and they were still locked in the chicken coop. Just some bloody feathers outside."

Fred was silent for a moment, his anger building. He was sure it was a weasel. It was just the way a weasel would kill, and one had already killed three of their chickens a week before. Those five chickens would have been good to eat later when they stopped laying, and their eggs were always needed to sell or to eat. He finished washing his hands and sat down at the dinner table.

"I better go look at that chicken coop this afternoon," Fred mumbled as he ate, but he hated to take time for it when he was cutting hay. Unexpected things could come up on the farm any day, and rarely did he have spare time to deal with them. The thought of a weasel hunt disturbed his dinner, but it didn't stop him from eating. He needed that good dinner of meat and potatoes for his afternoon work.

When dinner was finished, Fred went out to the chicken coop. He saw a small crack along the base of the wall, possibly big enough for the weasel to squeeze through. He found a piece of scrap wood and nailed it over the crack as a quick fix, but he wasn't sure it would keep the weasel out. Out in the orchard, he dug a pit and buried the two dead chickens deep enough that the roaming dogs and raccoons wouldn't dig them up.

The sweet smell of newly cut hay turned Fred's mind away from the weasel to filling the barn for winter and feeding a couple of beautiful, white-faced steers that would soon feed the family. In late afternoon, he finished cutting hay and put the horses away in time for supper. Later it would be time to slop the hogs and milk the cows. By bedtime, he had completely forgotten the weasel and the dead chickens.

Emma went to gather eggs the next day, and Fred was happy to hear that no more chickens had been killed. He hoped he had stopped the weasel with his repair work, but he wondered where the weasel had gone and what it would do next. He gave the matter little thought; weasels and dogs and other small animals were not his biggest concerns. He had a farm to run and a family to take care of.

Right after the morning milking, a car pulled into the barnyard. It was Fred's nephew Art Glecker, who lived just down the road.

"Wanta do that roofing on the corncrib today, Fred?" Art asked as he got out of the car.

The two of them had agreed that at the first sign of good weather and a break in the field work, they would start re-roofing the corncrib. Fred remembered and glanced up at the aging shingles.

"Yep. Looks like this is the day," Fred replied. "I guess I can't sit all day under the shade tree and drink lemonade."

"No, I guess you can't sit in the shade, not today," said Art, knowing how absurd it was to think of Fred sitting in the shade for more than a few minutes any day. "I'll get the ladder and hammers ready."

While Fred put the filled milk cans in the cool water in the tiny milk house, Art got out the tall ladder and leaned it against the corncrib. The two of them hauled two bundles of wooden shingles to the roof and nailed down a rail to keep them from sliding off as they worked. They began hammering down the new shingles, part of a row at a time.

The sound of the hammers echoed off the house, making a pleasing sound of work above the flat, quiet farmland. The rhythm gave Emma a feeling of progress and security as she worked in the kitchen. It pleased her to think of the men at work and know that she and Fred were working together, though separately.

It was still only mid-morning when something caught Fred's eye at the peak of the roof. He glanced up and saw nothing, but the flash of something came again a few seconds later. That time he saw it. It was the weasel! There it came, wobbling over the peak of the roof, right toward Art. It looked unsteady and sick, and it looked completely fearless.

"Art! Look out!" Fred yelled.

Art whirled around just in time to see the weasel pause above him. It wavered and then started a hopping, weird dash down the roof toward him. In an instant, Art raised his hammer and threw it at the weasel, hitting it in the head. The force of the hammer blow spun the weasel around. The weasel and the hammer slid off the roof to the ground. Both men yelled.

"Get him, didja?" Fred yelled. "You okay?"

"I'm okay, but he ain't," Art said. "I couldna made that throw again if my life depended on it."

"Well, yer life *did* depend on it that time!" Fred yelled. "He musta had the rabies. I never seen a weasel out in daytime like that, and to attack a man! He was crazy with the rabies!"

The two men climbed down to look at the weasel. It was dead, and there was blood on the fur around its head and front paws. There was also a ring of white foam around its mouth.

"Good thing it didn't get to bite ya," Fred said.

"Yep, good thing. We better bury him pretty deep."

Emma came running out. "What's wrong? What's wrong? I heard you yellin'! Did one of you fall off the roof?"

"No. We're okay. Looky here. We got your weasel!"

"Oh! You got him! Good! How'd you do it, Fred?"

"Art did it. You shoulda seen him throw that hammer!"

They told her all about the wobbly weasel trying to attack them and how Art had killed it with his hammer. Emma shook her head again and again. "The Lord really protected you," she said softly. She knew rabies was incurable, and it gave her a fright. She quickly looked up and offered a prayer. "Thank you, Lord, for protecting these men from the weasel and the rabies!"

Art nodded his approval and said, "Amen."

Fred just looked down at the weasel and at his shoes and then sheepishly at Emma. Fred hadn't been in church for a long time, and Emma did the praying at their house. It seemed like she prayed about everything. He didn't disagree with her prayer, but it seemed out of place. Art was the one that killed the weasel, and he didn't need prayer to do it, Fred thought.

Emma went back inside, and Fred got a shovel and scooped up the weasel. The two men took the weasel to the edge of the cornfield and buried it deep enough to keep rabies from spreading through some scavenging animal that might dig it up.

As they buried the weasel, Art thought about a farmer near Gibsonburg who had been bitten by a rabid dog. The man had writhed in bed and foamed at the mouth. After nearly two weeks, the man died. Art shuddered.

"That was quite a time," Art said when they were finished.

"Yep," Fred allowed. "Make a good story to tell the kids when they get home from school. They might tell the others at school. Don't see nothing like that very often."

Fred was right. His kids told other kids at school. Fred's kids told their children years later and they told *their* kids. The story still hasn't been forgotten even though most people don't think about a weasel unless they hear that children's song that says, "Pop goes the weasel!"

(A weasel is a long, thin varmint known mostly for its ability to squeeze into even the smallest opening in a chicken coop. They are like vampires, sucking blood from their victims. Weasels in Ohio have fur the same color as a red fox. We kids used to sing these words when we played in the yard: "Round and round the vinegar jug, the monkey chased the weasel; the monkey thought was all in fun. Pop! Goes the weasel." Art really popped the weasel that day.

Fred didn't join in the prayer that day, and he stayed away from church for many more years. Near the end of his life, he turned to God and prayed for forgiveness for ignoring God so long.)

6
Robbers in the Night

———✦———

IT HAD FELT LIKE SNOW all day. The sky was heavy and gray, and the air was damp and cold. In 1921, there were no reliable weather forecasts, even though weather observation stations had been communicating weather reports by telegraph since the mid-1800s and later by telephone and then radio. These reports helped but did not provide accurate forecasts. Most people just learned to judge by the feel of the air and the look of the sky and hoped they were right.

Fred Kardatzke was bringing in the last two buckets of milk near sundown when the snow began. It started fast, like sharp pebbles, first bouncing on the gravel and then settling on it and covering it. He turned his face a little to the east, away from the wind, and walked faster to the milk house. He shut the door while he poured the milk into the ten-gallon collection cans floating in cold water. By the time he was done with his final chore of the day, the storm had gained energy, and he was glad to reach the house before it hit with full force.

"Gonna be a real blizzard," he said to Emma as he came in, his coat loaded with snow pebbles.

"Yep. I seen it comin', and I hoped you'd git in fast," she replied without looking up from her cooking.

He left his boots and coat in the mud porch and took a cup from the cupboard. Hot coffee was always good at a time like this.

"Where the kids?" he asked.

"Some in there and some upstairs," she said, nodding toward the living room. "They got their studies to do."

He looked in and could see three of the youngest, sprawled on the floor with their books near the heat register. Recently he had installed a large coal-burning furnace in the cellar that warmed the downstairs and sent a little heat drifting up the stairs to the kids' bedrooms. The kids didn't look up when he came in but kept reading, so he thought it best not to start any talk with them just then. Time enough for that at supper. Anyhow, he didn't want to talk about their schoolwork. A little of that went a long way for him. He slipped into his chair for another look at last Sunday's paper. It was the main thing he read, and the Sunday paper usually lasted him all week.

Elmer, the youngest boy, noticed his father and broke the silence. "Pa, do you think we'll have school tomorrow if it snows really hard?"

Fred was a little annoyed at the question. The one-room school was right across the road from their house. Why wouldn't they have school? Of course, there was the little matter of the schoolteacher getting there.

"I dunno," he said. "Depends on whether Miss Wainwright can make it out from town." He thought for a minute and added, "Course, if she can't come, I could come and teach you kids a thing or two!"

All the kids laughed at that idea. "Would you really teach school?" one of the little girls yelled. All of them laughed again, and Fred laughed a little, too, and shook his head.

The kids knew Pa only visited the school a couple of times each year, unless one of them got in trouble. He had only gone to eighth grade when he was a boy, and he didn't understand why any of his kids needed to go further than he had. Carl and Harris were already in high school, and there might be more of that kind of thing soon. The way Carl talked about school all the time convinced him he hadn't heard the last on that topic.

"Supper's ready," Emma announced. "I need some help in here."

Pa didn't like his supper to be served cool or late. Three of the kids hopped up, ready to move around and make sure suppertime was a happy time. When all the family had gathered around the kitchen table, all eleven of them, Ma asked Harris, the oldest boy, to pray. When he finished his prayer, the food began to disappear.

There wasn't a lot of talk around the table. Pa didn't like to hear a lot of talk when he was eating. But when the wind blew hard against the house and snow pelted the windows, Ma said, "Sounds pretty bad out there. Good thing we got the new coal furnace."

After supper, three of the girls helped Ma in the kitchen. Two of the older boys bundled up in their coats and went to the barn with Pa to make sure the animals were inside and the doors were all shut. This evening would be a bad time for a cow or pig to go wandering.

Back in the house, it was bright and warm. The checkerboard was out, and so was the carrom board. Expert fingers would soon be flicking the wooden shooter carrom rings, hitting the red and green rings into the corner pockets to earn the right to shoot in the black ring for added points. Many snowy nights were enlivened by checkers, carroms, Old Maid, other card games, and popcorn.

An evening of fun began. The click of the carrom rings and the tapping of checkers measured off the time before bedtime. Pa checked the furnace one more time, shook out the ashes, and added more coal. When he came back upstairs, he announced, "Pert near bedtime," and looked around the kitchen and living room to see if all the kids had heard.

They had all heard, and they had learned that it was best to listen whenever Pa made one of his announcements. The games were put away, and the race was on for the stairs. Pa ignored the thunder of feet and turned off lamps in the living room. As he did, he thought about how fortunate they were to be the first people on their road to have electricity. Their house was near the state route that ran along the river, and the electric poles came only as far as their house.

Quiet settled in for the night. Chatter and giggling ended upstairs. The only sound was the moaning of the winter storm. Fred and Emma prepared for bed in their own ways. It would be good to settle down under the blankets and let the storm blow itself out. As he pulled thick blankets over his shoulders, Fred began to think about the animals in the barn and the other buildings. He could see himself checking them in the morning, and soon he drifted into sleep and dreams.

Soon after they fell asleep, a shot of fear went through Fred and he was awake. Then he remembered his dream. What remained of it was mainly a feeling, but in the dream, he had seen dark figures coming to the house. Even awake, he felt overwhelming fear. He was sure the dream figures were robbers. It was a warning.

He sat up in bed, awake with the fear of death. After listening for a minute, he lay back down.

"What is it, Fred?" Emma asked.

"They're coming," he said, almost in a whisper.

"Who's coming?" she asked.

"Robbers. I dreamed that robbers are coming."

They both listened, and all they heard was the wind outside. She was about to tell him it was just a dream when a wave of fear swept over both of them. They lay motionless and listened. No! They could hear men's voices just outside the house! It must be the robbers!

Emma and Fred didn't move, and the voices came closer. Soon feet were stomping on the side porch, and there was a loud knock on the door.

Fred thought about his shotgun, but it was at the other end of the house, and he didn't know if he had any shells. It was a crazy thought, he knew, but his fear was taking him over. He should just find out who was there. Maybe his dream was wrong. Maybe they were neighbors needing help.

"Stay here," he said to Emma as he put on his heavy gray sweater and went to the door. She could hear him open the door and begin talking with someone. When she heard him say, "Well, better come on in," she got up quickly and put on a warm housecoat. In the kitchen light she could see two men, quite young and unknown to her. They weren't dressed for the cold. They were so poorly dressed that it seemed as though a careless mother had dressed them. She looked at Fred for an explanation.

"They got car trouble," Fred told her. "Car slid in the ditch down the road. I kin get 'em out in the morning. Have enough blankets for 'em to sleep on the floor?"

Emma looked the men over, and they seemed like just big boys, not much older than her older sons.

"Sure, we got blankets," she said and went to pull them out of the back closet. They always had extra blankets because it was common to have relatives drop in for the night. They had no extra beds, so the kids would usually sleep on the floor and let the company have their beds. This time the visitors would sleep on the floor.

Fred talked only a little with the men while Emma made them beds on the floor. He never liked to talk much, and he especially didn't like to talk in the middle of the night with strangers he thought might be robbers. He looked them over carefully while they talked, and they seemed like simple town boys. They didn't seem to be armed or dangerous, and it was clear they were grateful to be in out of the storm. They told Fred they had gotten lost on their way to Toledo. He wondered why they were out there on the country road during a storm and why so late at night.

When Emma finished making beds of blankets on the floor for the men, she said, "We don't have pillows. Can you sleep without pillows?"

The men looked at each other and at her. "Sure," they said with a shrug.

"We all better git to bed," Fred said, making his words sound like a warning. "My wife cooks a good breakfast, but she cooks it early."

The house was quiet again, and the only sound was the storm. Fred didn't fall asleep so quickly this time. Thoughts continued to bother him. What if they really were robbers? What if the dream was true?

He thought he was still awake thinking about robbers all night when he heard a pan in the kitchen and smelled coffee. Emma was frying some ham from the hog they had butchered two weeks earlier. It was still dark and would be for a time, but it was time to get up, nearly five o'clock in the morning. Fred pulled on his shirt and overalls and walked in his socks to the kitchen. Emma set a cup of coffee on the table, and he sat down to put on his shoes. They looked at each other and then toward the living room, but they didn't speak. They didn't want to wake up the sleepers.

The next sounds they heard were squeaks from the floor upstairs. Some of the kids had smelled the ham and were up. Sometimes they were noisy in the morning, but today the first ones awake were getting up quietly.

Fred watched as Lucille and Forrest entered the living room and stopped. They looked at the sleeping bodies on the floor and then tiptoed around the mysterious guests to the kitchen.

"Who is that?" Lucille whispered. "Are they the cousins from Michigan?"

Emma had sisters in Michigan, and their kids were among the favorite visitors.

"No, those are no cousins of yours," Ma said. "We don't even know who they are."

The words startled the children. They looked at their mother and then again at the sleepers.

"Why are they here?" Forrest asked.

"Car slid in the ditch in the storm last night," Ma explained and kept fixing breakfast. "Musta been ten o'clock when they come knockin' on the door. Pa let 'em in to sleep here. He's gonna git their car out after breakfast."

The kids quickly tiptoed to the south windows to see the car in the ditch. Sure enough, there it was, halfway to the river. They scampered upstairs to tell the other kids the exciting news. "Strangers are sleeping downstairs! Their car is in the ditch! They came in the middle of the night and slept here! Come down and see them!"

Emma heard the commotion upstairs, so she hurried breakfast along. Soon all the kids came down the stairs, making a noise like rolling thunder. Like Lucille and Forrest had done earlier, the others stopped in their tracks and fell silent when they saw the bodies on the floor. Then all nine of them crept through the living room and past the sleepers, looking them over cautiously.

Emma put a finger over her mouth to tell them to stay quiet, and they slipped into their places at the table. The ham and eggs and bread were disappearing when a man appeared silently at the living room door to the kitchen. Everyone was startled that he had made his way there so quietly.

"Well, did ya sleep okay?" Ma asked the stranger, who replied with a nod of his head.

Pa didn't say anything. He just looked at the young man suspiciously. The dream of robbers was still on his mind, but how could he tell if somebody was a robber by looking at him? He particularly didn't like the looks of this one. He was skinny with blond hair and pale eyebrows that made him look like a criminal. *Just like me,* he thought when he realized the young man looked something like he had at that age. That thought didn't decrease his dislike for the man.

"How 'bout wakin' up your friend and havin' breakfast?" Ma offered. "Then you'll both have time to eat before for our morning worship."

No one in the family was surprised at Emma's announcement. She always led them in worship after breakfast with prayer, a Bible verse, a song, and sometimes even her version of a little sermon.

Fred felt a little embarrassed and thought, *What would these men think when they had to "go to church" for their breakfast?* Then he thought, *What do I care? It serves them right to have church with their breakfast after waking us up in the middle of the night. If they are robbers, Emma's little "church service" will be just what they need.*

Although he sat through it for the sake of his wife, Fred was never really in the spirit of morning worship. Her brother George Gleckler got saved and became a Christian after a family tragedy, the train accident that had killed his wife and son. The church that formed as a result of the Gleckler family tragedy met in several homes in the area, and Emma was one of its most active leaders. She thought and talked about God and the church every chance she had. Fred knew she wouldn't miss this chance.

The other man appeared at the kitchen door, and Fred decided he didn't like his looks either. His brown hair was rumpled, and he had a dishonest, shifty way of looking around the kitchen. He thought again about his dream.

The kids slid their chairs aside, and two of the older boys brought extra chairs from the mud porch. The strangers were placed side by side at the end of the table, facing Fred. Plates of food were handed to them, and it seemed they hadn't eaten for a while. The children noticed their poor manners but kept their eyes on their own plates. Fred noticed everything.

After the table was cleared, Emma started morning worship with a short prayer of thanks for breakfast and shelter from the storm. She gave thanks that the mysterious visitors had found safety in the family's house and had not frozen in the storm, going out into eternity in whatever their spiritual condition might be. Then Emma asked Lucille to read a short passage from the Old Testament about the Ten Commandments, after which she told a short version of the story of the prodigal son. To end, everyone sang "The Way of the Cross Leads Home," and then Emma asked Harris to give the closing prayer.

Fred kept watching the two visitors, who were barely older than his boys. Both looked down at the table most of the time, only peeking around the room a few times. He thought they probably never had to sit through morning worship at the breakfast table before.

"I guess we better see if we kin git that car outa the ditch," Fred announced. Then he thought he would quiz the boys a little.

"You boys brothers?" he asked.

"Just friends," the blond one said.

"Where ya from?"

"Toledo."

"Whatya doin' way out here?"

"Seein' friends in Oak Harbor," the dark-haired boy answered.

"Oak Harbor? I know lots of people in Oak Harbor. Maybe I know your friends there," Fred replied. He thought the boys became pale when he said that.

"Well, they don't exactly live in Oak Harbor anymore but nearby," the blond one said nervously.

"What're their names?" Fred pressed.

After a pause, the blond-haired one said the most common name he could think of. "Johnson. Tom Johnson and his family."

"How long you known the Johnsons?" Fred pressed him.

"Long time. My folks knew them in Toledo," the shifty boy answered.

Fred thought for a minute. He was sure the name wasn't real, but he thought it best not to press the issue further. Anyway, if the friends didn't live there anymore, why did that blond-haired one say they'd seen them in Oak Harbor?

"I hope I get to meet them sometime," he said after a minute. "I'll ask about them next time I'm in Oak Harbor."

Everyone got up from the table, and the children went to find their warmest clothes. Fred got his boots and coat from the mud porch. He wasn't going to leave these men in the house with his family, so he said, "You can come with me to hitch up the horses. They can probably pull your car out of that little ditch. Ennaway, I don't think the tractor will start in this cold."

Before Fred and the men left the house, Emma came in from the living room with two gospel tracts. Giving one to each of the young men, she said, "Take these with you and read them. They will tell you the way of salvation."

The men looked at her sheepishly and tucked the tracts into their pockets. One of them mumbled, "Thank you, ma'am."

Fred burned with embarrassment and pushed his way out the door.

Emma watched the two young men follow Fred to the barn. In a few minutes, the wide barn doors opened, and the big team of horses emerged. Their breath made small clouds in the cold air, and she thought they were beautiful to see.

The men and horses trudged through the snow out to the road. The snow wasn't very deep, and most of it had blown off the road near the car. Emma moved around to the south-facing windows to watch the car come out of the ditch. By this time, the children were dressed and joined her.

"Looks like ya just drove off the road," Fred observed at the car. "Couldn't see the edge in the snow?"

The boys both shook their heads. "We thought we were in the middle of the road. We couldn't back out when we drove in there."

Fred moved the horses past the car and attached a long chain to the rear bumper. It wouldn't take much to pull the car out of the shallow ditch.

"See if you can start it," he told the boys. The dark-haired one got in, and the car started with no trouble.

"Okay, when I say go, you back up the car but make sure you stop when you're out of the ditch. I don't want you runnin' over my horses," Fred ordered.

They could see it would be best to follow this man's instructions exactly and not run over his horses.

Fred urged the horses forward until the chain was tight. "Okay! Go!" he yelled, and the driver started backing the car out of the ditch. The horses leaned into their collars and pulled, and the car was soon up on the road. It hadn't seemed hard at all to these huge draft horses. Fred unhooked the chain and turned the horses back toward the barn.

"If you're goin' to Toledo, you can go on up this road to the first big road. That's 163. Turn left, and you can find your way to Woodville Road," Fred said.

The two men nodded, looked up the road, and then down at their feet. Their shiftiness heightened Fred's suspicions.

"Thanks, mister," one of them said, and they climbed quickly into the car and started up the road.

The car looked too good for those scruffy young men, Fred thought as they drove away. He made his way back to the barn, put the horses away, and went back to the house to get a better coat.

"Whatcha doin', Pa?" Emma asked.

"I'm goin' to town. I gotta see the police. Them men were too suspicious." Emma shuddered when he added, "My dream was right. They were robbers."

Fred was glad that his car, inside the corncrib, started easily. The snow had stopped, so he drove carefully into town with no trouble. Elmore had a small police station, but it wasn't open all the time. He went there first. To his surprise, he found local policeman Ernie Sondergeld there. He described his night's adventure, the men, and the car they were driving.

"That's them, alright," Ernie said. "They stole that car in Oak Harbor. I got a call last night. Which way did they go?"

"They went north on my road. I told 'em how to go to Toledo," Fred explained.

"We'll get 'em," Ernie said. "Toledo police are already lookin' for 'em." He reached for his big black phone and placed the call and talked in serious tones. When he put down the phone, he turned to Fred.

"You have any other trouble with them boys?" he asked.

"Like what?" Fred asked.

"Well, it sounds like them same two got pretty rough with a man at a gas station in Oak Harbor. Hit him and stole some gas too," Ernie said.

Fred felt the chill of fear he had felt the night before. "No, pretty peaceful at my house," he said.

"Well, we'll get 'em," Ernie said. "We'll get 'em."

As Fred drove back to the farm, he wondered what would happen to those young men. He didn't know much about the police or the courts or the prisons. He didn't know how long they would be in prison if they had to go there. At last he was getting over his fear, and he was surprised to be feeling sorry for the boys. He hoped they wouldn't be in prison too long. He felt sorry for their parents too. Then he remembered the tracts Emma had given them and the morning worship she made them listen to.

Maybe it was the right thing to do, he thought. *Maybe they still have a chance to go right. They can even read the tracts in prison.*

Work on the farm started as usual that day with the morning milking. Leta Wainright, the schoolteacher, made it out to the Leatherport School from town on the interurban, so there were classes all day for the school-age children.

At supper that evening, the kids asked, "Who were those men at breakfast?"

Emma looked at Fred to answer. "Well, it turns out they were robbers," he said. "They stole that car. They were car thieves."

The kids gasped. "Robbers! How did you find out, Pa?" one of them asked.

"I went to town and told the police," Fred said. "They were already looking for them and the car they stole."

The kids asked many more questions about the men, the car, the police, and the danger of robbers coming to the house. Nothing like this had ever happened to them before. Pa said the men would probably go to prison, and the kids at first appeared to feel safer, but then they felt sad, imagining what it would be like to go to prison. Emma sensed their thoughts.

"The worst thing about it is that those men aren't saved," she said. "If they were, they wouldn't a done a thing like that. At least we had a chance to witness to 'em. I gave 'em tracts about salvation before they left."

The children looked at their mother. She had witnessed to the two robbers who had come in the night, robbers who might have robbed them if they'd had a chance. *Ma is a good woman,* they thought, *a good Christian woman. And Pa did right too.*

(My father, Arlin Kardatzke, told me about this incident in detail in the late 1900s, including his father's dream about the robbers. Arlin was probably about ten years old at the time, so the incident happened around 1921. The game of carrom mentioned here, or carroms, is a form of billiards or table shuffleboard. It's played on a board about three feet square with net pockets in the corners. The players flick shooter [or "striker"] rings against the red and green rings called carroms. The player who first clears the board of his colored rings may shoot the black or red ring called the queen. The game originated in India and became popular in the United States after World War I.)

Fred Kardatzke home in the 1940s.

The Fred Kardatzke home after a winter storm; the milk house is in the center; the former Leatherport School is on the right. Segments of the house were added separately. The wing on the left was built in the 1860s.

Part Two

The Interurban Train Line: Speed and Danger

7
Interurban History

---⚜---

LEATHERPORT WAS CONNECTED TO nearby cities and towns by an interurban train line. It was like a city streetcar except that it ran across the countryside between cities and small towns on standard-gauge railroad tracks. Like a streetcar, the interurban stopped at farms and crossroads along its path. Interurbans connected towns and neighborhoods that didn't have regular train lines before automobile travel became common.

The interurban train line that ran through Leatherport had the grander, more official name of "The Toledo, Port Clinton, and Lakeside Railway" (TPC&L), but it was known around Leatherport simply as "the interurban." It had a stop in downtown Leatherport and at most highway intersections on its path. It ran south from Toledo to Elmore, then turned east and traveled on the north side of the Portage River through Oak Harbor and farther east to Port Clinton. It terminated farther east at Marblehead, Ohio. The

TPC&L operated for fifty-three years, from 1905 until 1958, carrying freight, gravel, coal, and farm products as well as passengers.

The historic timetable records show that the trains regularly ran at speeds over 60 miles per hour, amazingly fast for any form of travel when the line was created. In its early glory years, the interurban took people from Toledo to summer vacation places on Lake Erie. After two hours and many stops, it arrived at Marblehead. From Marblehead, passengers could take a ferryboat to Cedar Point, the great amusement park that opened in 1870. The TPC&L was more profitable than most interurbans, but by 1939 it had ceased passenger service, and freight service ended in 1958. Paved roads, cars, and trucks doomed it and nearly all the other interurban lines.

Rollin Gleckler, my dad's cousin, saw the tracks being laid in 1905 when he was a young boy, and he saw the tracks being pulled up again when he was an old man. It had its glory days, but it also had dangers known only to those living alongside its tracks.

Passenger hailing the interurban near Elmore, Ohio.

8
Death and Danger

JUST WEST OF LEATHERPORT was a notorious curve in the interurban's tracks called "Linker's Curve." The train tracks were laid to swoop out around Mr. Linker's barn to avoid separating the barn from the owner's house. When a train was passing behind the barn, the conductor's view of the track beyond the barn was blocked, so an oncoming train could come into sight unexpectedly at very close range.

Two serious train wrecks happened in the history of the TPC&L Railway, and they both happened on Linker's Curve, just east of the barn, where you can still see power lines in the field. Twice trains collided head-on there. In both cases, the conductors had ignored the right-of-way signals and had gone speeding along, heedless of the blind spot ahead. One man died in the first collision.

The danger to people who lived along the track was very real to my father. Before I was born, my parents lived in one half of a rented two-story brick house right in Leatherport, about a half mile east of Linker's Curve. My father was a young farmer then. The house was on the river side of the interurban train tracks, but the barn and cattle and fields were on the north side, across the tracks. It was the very arrangement that William Linker had avoided by having the tracks curve around his barn. A similar arrangement had not been possible at the old Wendt place where my parents lived. The deep gulley at the end of Graytown Road made it impossible to bend the track out around the barn.

Every day my father had to cross the road and the interurban tracks to feed and milk his cows. One evening he was carrying two buckets of milk from the barn, heading for the house across the tracks. He didn't hear the interurban train coming, and he didn't see it in the blinding light of the setting sun. Just as he crossed the tracks, he saw the train and heard its whistle. Instead of hurrying on across the track to the house, he panicked, turned, and jumped back across the track toward the barn. The train whistle shrieked, and the front of the car just missed him. As it went roaring past, startled passengers and the conductor looked out the windows, wondering why the farmer was so close to the tracks when their train went racing by.

(A newer barn now stands at Linker's Curve, but the power lines in the field follow the long-abandoned line of the interurban.)

9
Sunday Derailment

One Sunday in about 1949, as my family was on the way home from church in Elmore, my dad slowed the car, pulled to the side, and stopped on River Road at the end of Graytown Road.

"Look at that!" my dad said.

We kids stopped chattering and looked where he was pointing. A small train engine and two gravel cars were sitting on the tracks right across our road, blocking our way home. We had never seen anything like it. How could such a big, powerful machine be stopped in its tracks, especially across our road?

"Looks like the interurban jumped the track while we were in church," my dad said. "We gotta go around the block to get home."

We lived out in the country, so I didn't know what "around the block" meant. In this case, it meant we had to turn around and travel on other roads for about two miles until we made it home. The detour made for a

Leatherport, Ohio

slightly later Sunday dinner that afternoon, but it was worth it because we had seen a derailed train.

(In 2019 the interurban station could be seen at the intersection of Route 51 and State Road 105 just north of Elmore. The small, white frame building was used for a time by the Girl Scouts after the interurban stopped running.)

10
The Legacy of the Interurban

As a young boy growing up in Leatherport, I saw some of the rolling stock on the interurban and later saw the tracks being taken up. The roadbed was graded and landscaped, and strangers now wouldn't guess there had ever been a railroad running through those lovely lawns. It was a wonderful surprise many years later to have this conversation in Los Angeles in 1968:

When I was a graduate student at UCLA, the economic history class had pizza one night after class in 1968 with our professor, George Hilton. The genial professor and I began talking.

"Where are you from?" Professor Hilton asked.

"Elmore, Ohio," I said, thinking I would have to tell him where Elmore is.

"Elmore, Ohio!" he exclaimed, "I know it well! I have walked the interurban line in both directions from Elmore!"

Professor Hilton explained that he had written about the history of the Toledo, Port Clinton, and Lakeside Railway in a small book by that title. He had explored the full length of the interurban train line and had actually tromped around its grassy grave of downtown Leatherport.

The UCLA professor knew more about the interurban and Leatherport than most people living near the train's line, including me.

Part Three

Swamp Draining

11
The Gleckler Tile Yard

DRAINING THE GREAT BLACK SWAMP began in the 1800s with a system of ditches to make the rich swampland dry enough for farming. Ditches carried surface water to the swamp's languid creeks and swales. By the late 1800s, the ditches were being augmented by rows of 4-inch clay drainage tiles laid in trenches four to six feet below farm fields. Surface water and deeper ground water oozed into the tiles and flowed through them to the nearest ditch and on to the river.

One of many small factories making drainage tiles was on the north edge of Leatherport on Graytown Road. Christopher Gleckler, one of my great-grandfathers, had brought his brick-making skills from Germany in 1860, and he started the factory in 1879. By the early twentieth century, the Gleckler Tile Yard was producing 4-inch field tiles, 12-inch clay main line tiles, bricks, and hollow tile block for buildings.

Tiles were made from the clay that lay just below the black topsoil in Leatherport. Workers scraped away the topsoil to mine the clay underneath. At the factory, the clay was formed into tiles that were dried and then fired in flaming kilns. The tiles went to farms nearby and to others many miles away. To local farm people, the tile factory was an amazing, fire-breathing, smoking spectacle right out there between fields of corn and beans.

Grim work in the Gleckler Tile Yard, about 1900.

Gleckler Tile Yard seen from the west,
looking toward Graytown Road about 1900.

The Gleckler Tile Yard fell victim to competition from other tile factories, and it closed in 1935. In 1943, my family moved to the house on Graytown Road next to the ponds the tile yard had left behind. By then, all that remained of the tile yard were remnants of the coal-fired kilns. The arched roofs of the kiln furnaces suggested ancient Roman ruins. The large pond was a soggy monument to all those who had drained the swamp and made the tile to keep it drained.

In 1948, my father, Arlin Kardatzke, and a neighbor, Earl Sandrock, drained the large pond and began improvements around the shoreline. They built an earthen dam to create two smaller ponds, one for each landowner. The dam allowed Arlin and Earl to control their own ponds separately as they saw fit.

(Besides field tile, the Gleckler Tile Yard also produced something called "hollow block," an oversized hollow brick about a foot long with a 4x4-inch space inside. These hollow blocks can be seen in the walls of the house on the north side of the pond at 940 South Graytown Road. An old storage building of the same kind of block sits farther from the road in the same area. It was once an icehouse where people could buy blocks of ice to take home to their iceboxes before refrigerators were invented.)

12

George Gleckler's Icehouse

"I scream, you scream,
We all scream for ice cream"
Author Unknown

WATER FROM THE TILE YARD PONDS was turned into refrigeration for the families of the Leatherport area. Before home refrigerators and ice production plants, icehouses were filled with ice cut from frozen rivers or ponds to preserve food in the hot summer months. Some of that ice could be used for making ice cream, a great reward on a hot summer day.

Cutting, collecting, and storing ice wasn't easy. To harvest it, hired men walked out on the pond and cut the ice into large blocks. They used large crosscut saws that would otherwise be used to cut logs into boards. They sawed blocks and hoisted them out to create a channel. The men used long wooden poles to push ice blocks into the channel and on to the icehouse.

George Gleckler invented a gasoline-powered conveyor to lift the 80-pound blocks of ice from the pond into the icehouse. At the bottom end of the conveyer, a long, narrow channel of metal dipped into the pond. The conveyor's top end reached up into a window high in the end of the icehouse near the peaked roof. Something like a large bicycle chain traveled inside the channel, pulling vertical paddles that caught the blocks of ice and dragged them up into the window. The huge ice blocks dropped dangerously near the men working inside.

Inside the icehouse, men used ice tongs to drag the blocks of ice and stack them in layers. They spread sawdust between each layer to keep the ice blocks from sticking together. When the icehouse was filled, more sawdust was piled over the top and along all sides of the ice to insulate it. The ice remained through the summer months until October or November when the weather cooled again.

In the 1940s, customers could still buy big blocks of ice from a small building just off Fremont Street in Elmore. Most people who bought it used it to cool a home icebox, still in use at the time in homes without refrigerators. My family sometimes bought a block of ice on the way home from church on Sunday. We kids would cool our feet on it in the back seat. In the afternoon, my dad would wrap the block of ice in a burlap bag and hammer it into small pieces with a large mallet made of a tree limb. By evening, the whole family and sometimes some cousins had that treat worth screaming for—ice cream.

(*George Gleckler's gasoline-powered ice conveyor was a valuable innovation, but gasoline engines weren't new then. The first one was patented in 1794. The first American internal combustion engine, what we have inside our cars and trucks, was designed in 1798. Still, George Gleckler's gasoline-powered ice conveyor was a valuable innovation and a Leatherport marvel. George Gleckler also designed an elevator to lift pallets of soft tile to shelves in the tile-drying shed.)*

The icehouse in recent times. The pump house was behind the icehouse.

13
The Pump House

THE POND AT THE GLECKLER TILE YARD flooded in winter, so it had to be drained every year in the spring before the tile factory could begin work. The water was pumped out by a huge paddle-box pump housed in a shed between the large pond and a smaller one behind the icehouse. The paddle-box pump, driven at first by a steam-powered tractor, could empty the large pond entirely in a day or two, chugging away night and day.

The paddle-box pump worked like a water wheel, but instead of water pushing a vertical wheel, water was pushed out of the pond through an inclined box. Boards were attached to cogwheel chains that ran on both sides of the box. The chains ran over cogwheel gears at each end of the box.

Water from the pond flowed through a tile into the deep, open concrete-walled pit. One end of the paddle box fit snugly inside the pit. The other end of the paddle box angled upward and over a small dam to empty water into another pond. Huge chains similar to bicycle chains wrapped around cogwheels on each side of the paddle box at both ends. The 4-foot-long paddle boards were bolted to the chains at each side of the box.

To run the pump, a farm tractor was attached to the paddle box by a wide, circular rubber and canvas belt that ran over a wide, flat-wheel pulley on the side of the tractor to another flat pulley on the side of the pump box. When the tractor engine was engaged, the belt moved, the gears turned, and the paddle-box boards were pulled through the box and up to the discharge channel. The water was pushed up and out, and the paddle boards circled around and dived down again into the water at the low end. The water that was pushed up and out of the box flowed over a spillway into the small pond making a cascade that was an Ohio version of a mountain waterfall. From there, the water flowed out to the roadside ditch and on down to the Portage River.

(In the earliest days of the Gleckler Tile Yard, a steam tractor may have driven the pond-draining pump. Gasoline-powered tractors were used by the early 1900s.)

14
Draining the Ponds in 1948

———————✤———————

WHEN THE GLECKLER TILE YARD closed in 1935, the Leatherport ponds began to return to their natural state. Moss covered much of the pond, and cattails grew around the shores. Cranes waded in the shallow water, feeding on small fish. Muskrats formed cattail dens and burrowed into the banks. Seaweed made green underwater canyons where the water surface was free of moss. After years of collecting leaves and silt, the ponds were returning to their primeval form as part of the Great Black Swamp.

In 1948, two ponds remained. A small pond of about an acre was hidden behind the icehouse on its south side. It was owned by the Schwemberger family that was living in George Gleckler's former house.

The large pond stretched west from Graytown Road into farm fields and north nearly to the barnyard on the former Gleckler property. To the south, the large pond reached almost to the icehouse and the pump house. The large pond covered about seven acres, including the inlet near Graytown Road beside my family's house. That inlet was lined with broken bricks and tiles from the former tile yard.

My father and Earl Sandrock owned the land bordering the pond, and they had plans for how to renovate it. It seemed wise to them to create a separate pond for each owner, but how could they separate their parts of the pond? About that time, an opportunity arose for both separating the ponds and enhancing the area.

The Ottawa County Board of Supervisors had decided to deepen and widen the part of the La Carpe Creek which ran north and south between Graytown Road and Stange Road, a north-south road to the east. Doing so would improve the drainage between the two roads and speed the flow of water from farther away. A shallow ditch in fields a half mile east of Graytown Road already followed the planned new path for the creek, but enormous amounts of soil and clay would have to be dug up and removed to create the new, deeper, wider channel. The governing board made it known that the excavated soil could be had for only the cost of hauling it away.

When my father and Earl Sandrock heard the news, they decided to work together to haul in truckloads of clay to build a dam between the parts of the pond they each owned. The small eastern inlet would be separated from the larger pond, and the two newly created ponds could be landscaped and beautified. They especially wanted to cover the broken bricks and tiles around the pond's shores.

To prepare for the pond improvements, Arlin and Earl first had to drain the large pond. Arlin owned the inlet portion near Graytown Road, and Earl owned the much larger portion to the west. Draining the pond would require an exceptionally large pump, and one was readily available. The paddle-box pump that had served the tile factory so well looked as though it might still work.

The two men examined the box pump and tested it briefly with Earl's tall International Harvester tractor. The pump still worked. Even the underground tile connection from the large pond to the pump was intact, so water would flow in freely when the pump was activated.

On the day the drainage began, the whole neighborhood gathered behind the icehouse to see a re-enactment of the pond-draining at the long-gone tile yard. Earl Sandrock lined up his big tractor and attached its belt wheel to the steel wheel on the far end of the paddle-box pump. The huge circular belt loop was nearly a foot wide. It was fastened over the pump house wheel and threaded over the wheel on the side of Earl's tractor. To keep the belt firmly in place, Earl twisted it to form a figure eight. When the belt was turning around the cogwheels, the crossover in the middle kept the pump running the right direction and kept the belt from flopping off the belt wheels.

Earl gently backed the tractor until the belt was taut and ready. "Well, Arlin, should we give 'er a try?" he yelled.

"Might as well!" Arlin yelled. "See if she still works."

Earl powered up the tractor's engine and engaged the power take-off. The big belt began to turn, and the paddles in the box climbed up the incline just as they had done years earlier. A cascade of water splashed over the concrete spillway into the small pond, and a current formed across the pond. Everyone clapped. Kids ran around to see the water dumping down the spillway into the small pond, and they could see it was pushing its way to the ditch, heading for the Portage River.

The crowd soon dispersed while the tractor continued its work. That night the three closest families could hear the tractor running, pumping away when they went to bed, and it was still running the next morning. After just that one night of pumping, the pond was already low. It was so shallow that soon the pump had no water to move. The inlet beside Arlin's house was nearly drained. The bottom of the larger part of the pond was dotted with only a few puddles.

Earl turned off his tractor and freed it from the belt it had turned all night. Only small pools remained in the acres of mud where the large pond had been. From the shore, we kids saw the backs of large carp swimming in the larger of those pools. Smaller fish flipped frantically in the smaller pools, doomed as they were. Between the pools were the bodies of fish that had been in the wrong places when the water receded.

Earl spotted two huge turtles. Their backs stood out like small islands in the mud. In his knee boots, he walked through the mud and picked up the prehistoric monsters by their tails. Each turtle's shell was about two feet long. Earl carried the turtles to my family's driveway, and Arlin brought out a garden hose and washed mud from the turtles. Their black, armor-plated shells shone, and someone took a picture of Earl Sandrock standing on the turtles' backs. The turtles weren't smiling, but everyone else was.

My mother had heard of turtle soup, and had a recipe, so she decided to have Arlin butcher one of the turtles for cooking. She put the lean meat from the ancient turtle in a large pan with salt and a few herbs and started boiling it. Many hours later, my mother declared the turtle meat not fit for human consumption. It was still very tough and stringy, and it had a pond-like smell. Those who tasted it did not ask for more.

When the La Carpe Creek digging began, Arlin and Earl hired truckers to haul load after load of the displaced dirt to the shores of their ponds. They hauled dirt to the far west side of the large pond to fill in a shallow bay. They dumped more dirt around the edges of the Graytown Road inlet to cover the broken tiles and brick from the old tile yard. The largest deposit of clay formed a dam that separated Arlin's pond from the larger one to the west. The former Great Black Swamp land then had three ponds: the new one on Graytown Road, the larger pond behind it, and the smaller pond behind the icehouse and pump house.

Building the dam and separating the new front pond from the larger one was only the beginning of the work to improve drainage of the general area between Graytown Road and Stange Road. The newly separated ponds were deepened, and the shores were landscaped. The front pond on Graytown Road was my family's pond exclusively, and my father began landscaping it, planting grass, and dotting it with maple trees. We kids sometimes served as "indentured servants," working off our room and board. Because we were churchgoers and knew our Bible stories, sometimes we felt we were like slaves in biblical Egypt with our father as Pharaoh.

The pond on my family's land became our private swimming hole, fishing spot, frog-hunting arena, and ice rink. Eventually it became a "public" swimming pool of sorts, and by the late 1990s, so many strangers came to use it that my mother insisted that my father close it. He put up a sign on the biggest cottonwood tree announcing that the pond was private property, no longer open to the public. The crowds dwindled, and the pond was mostly unused except on weekends, when the grandchildren came and splashed into it.

In the 1990s, my older brother Merl bought the old family property, and their pond become a genteel lily pad pond, more fitting for the former city dwellers from Chicago. The small pond you can see on Graytown Road is a quiet place now, a gift from the ancient Gleckler Tile Yard's gift to modern Leatherport.

(You can visit the deep north-south section of the La Carpe Creek if you take the dirt road Township Highway 61, named DeWitt Road, that runs between Route 105 and Route 163 a half mile east of Graytown Road. The DeWitt Road may be a tongue-in-cheek reference to DeWitt Clinton, a promoter of the Erie Canal.)

Part Four

Prussian Progenitors

15
Frederick August Kardatzke

IF WE WERE TO BE TOTALLY HONEST about it, many of us who lived in and around Leatherport would have to admit we have Prussian ancestors. By Prussia, I mean that warlike area of Eastern Germany that had so much to do with unification of the German nation. It also had a lot to do with the Franco-Prussian War of 1870, World War I, and World War II. Prussia had a bad reputation for starting wars, and when our ancestors descended on the Great Black Swamp, it, too, fell prey to the warlike impulses of our family members and other Prussians.

To early Prussian settlers in the 1800s, the Great Black Swamp was an enemy to be attacked, conquered, inhabited, and endowed with the blessings of German American civilization. The stinking swamp water had to be drained. Foot-sucking muck had to be dried and turned into fertile farm soil. Swarming insects had to be deprived of nesting places, and other living creatures needed to be hunted and trapped and eaten, almost to the brink of extinction.

My grandfather, Frederick August Kardatzke (1883–1949), was the closest to an ancestral Prussian whom I knew personally, and he was only slightly tainted by the warlike strain in his Prussian genes. I knew him as a friendly, protective grandpa who had pink and white mint lozenges for me in the kitchen and always welcomed me in the milking shed. He even had a pig that was tame enough for his grandkids to ride. My memories of Grandpa Kardatzke have been shaped into colorful and entertaining stories you'll see later in this book.

16
Coming to Leatherport

CASTALIA, OHIO, IS THE FIRST KNOWN home of the Kardatzke family in this country. August Kardatzke, the first of the family name to appear on these shores, arrived in Ohio in May 1869. Over the next decade, his wife and nine adult children followed him across the salty waves. August died nineteen years later in a white frame farmhouse that may still be standing next to railroad tracks two or three miles east of Graytown, Ohio.

One of August's granddaughters told me of August's death. She was sleeping upstairs in the house on the night August Kardatzke died in 1892. The whole household was awakened by the news. At daybreak, men were already sawing and hammering to make a casket. At noon, they hailed an eastbound train and some of the men carried the casket bearing August's body into a luggage car. Two men accompanied the casket to Castalia, August's first American hometown. He was buried in the Castalia cemetery in a grave that is well marked to this day.

Leatherport, Ohio

Black Swamp drainage was well underway when Frederick Kardatzke was born at the tiny village of Vickery near Castalia in 1883. The only Castalia story that has come down through our immediate family is of Frederick's journey from Castalia to Leatherport in 1888 at the age of five. The train from Castalia to Elmore crossed Sandusky Bay on a stone causeway raised only a few feet above the water. Little Frederick looked out the passenger car windows on both sides and saw only water. He was terrified, feeling the train was plunging into deep water. When solid ground appeared on both sides of the car, his terror of the water and travel did not leave him.

Frederick's fear of travel lasted a lifetime. Perhaps because of his harrowing 30-mile train journey from Castalia to Leatherport, he became a lifelong stay-at-home. It is known that he sometimes drove his delivery truck to Pemberville, Ohio, thirteen miles to the west to deliver tile for the Gleckler Tile Yard. When he returned home after any of those epic journeys, he invariably reported to his wife Emma, "Well, I been all the way to Pemberville today."

Fred also went to Cedar Point on the Fourth of July each year, leaving his wife and nine children to celebrate on the farm. Pictures aren't available to confirm this, but he may have worn a shirt and tie for his annual trips to the pleasure capital of Northern Ohio. No stories have survived from his trips to Cedar Point, but there have been no hints that he was anything other than a model Prussian farmer out for a little fun on the Fourth of July.

His only known trip outside Ohio was in 1931 to attend his son Carl's wedding in Chicago.

(I have always wondered if one motivation for August's exit from Prussia was to keep his sons out of Bismarck's armies.

Castalia was known for the Blue Hole, a huge spring of fresh, cold water. It attracted tourists year-round until the 1970s when the owners closed it to the public in the wake of exorbitantly expensive handicap accessibility regulations. It's now a trout farm and private fishing club.

Endearing stories about Fred Kardatzke are scattered throughout this book, and there's more about him in one of my previous books, The Clock of the Covenant.*)*

17
Harman Kardatzke

───✠───

THE TEMPERAMENT OF ONE Prussian can serve as an example of the men who drained the swamp in the 1800s and kept it drained. That man was Harman Kardatzke (1862–1941), my great-grandfather. If I ever met Harman, I was one year old. I don't remember the experience.

Harman was born in 1862 near Stolp, Prussia. He was a mere boy at the time of the Franco-Prussian War in 1870–71, so he can't be blamed for it. He came to the United States as a ten-year-old in 1872. His childhood was probably like that of most farm children in the late 1800s, filled with hard work from an early age and rough play in adolescence. Those who knew Harman never accused him of being a fun-loving, easy-going guy. His father, August Kardatzke, may have been as stern as Harman or more so.

Photos of Harman Kardatzke in adult life show him as a serious, determined-looking man. Sometimes he is clean-shaven. In other photos he has a bushy mustache like that sported by Otto von Bismarck, the autocrat credited with German unification in 1871. I prefer to think of Harman as my family's very own Bismarck, but Harman was a stern warrior who battled weeds and swamp water in Ohio when he might have preferred warfare in Europe. In his photos, he is not smiling.

Only a few glimpses of Harman Kardatzke have percolated down to me, but they may be enough to give you a glimpse of this formidable Prussian ancestor.

Harman in a black vest strikes a defiant pose.

18
A Burning Barn

---※---

ONE EARLY STORY INVOLVING Harman must have happened in about 1926. At the time, my father was a teenager and a member of his grandfather Harman's work crew.

That summer Harman was leading a tiling crew that was laying field tile somewhere on a farm on Graytown Road. The team probably had a gasoline-powered tractor and a trenching machine. The trenching machine chewed a narrow trench about 15 inches wide and about 4 to 5 feet deep. As the trench was being dug, one man sat on a small wooden sled inside the newly dug trench, directly behind the huge trenching wheel. He laid the field tiles end to end as the machine crept forward. Tiny gaps between the tiles allowed water to seep in and flow through the tiles to the ditch at the end of the row and on to the Portage River.

The man in the trench who laid the tile was supported by two or three men and a team of horses that brought tiles to the edge of the trench. One of the men handed tiles down to the man in the trench. The newly tiled trench would be covered a few days later by men with a horse and a hand-guided earth scraper. It was all backbreaking work.

Tiling work began each day as soon as the men finished their morning chores, and it continued through the day with occasional breaks for rest and drinks of water, dinner at noon, and supper in early evening. As the sun was about to set and Harman's exhausted workers wanted to quit for the day, he was known to say in his heavy Prussian accent, "Yust vun morr rrott, boys! Yust vun morr rrott!" The weary workers would then straighten, look at the setting sun, and lay another sixteen and a half feet of tile: one rod.

At sunset on one of those evenings, my father looked across the fields and saw a barn ablaze about a mile away. Forgetting his tile-laying duties, he bolted for home, grabbed his Kodak box camera, mounted his bike, and rode to the fire. He somehow steadied his box camera on top of a fence post and took a time exposure photo of the burning barn. The black-and-white photo remains in the Kardatzke archives.

I don't know if my father returned to tiling that night, risking his grandfather's wrath. By the time he took the picture, the tiling crew probably would have finished work for the day, and Harman would have had the night to rest and cool his temper.

(Fields around the Leatherport area are still drained by a labyrinth of underground tiles.)

The barn that burned.

19
Knife Throwing

---※---

OLD-TIME PRUSSIANS ATE SOME of their supper off wide table knives like the spatula you might use to spread cake icing. Harman was, in fact, an old-time Prussian, so it was natural for him to crowd potatoes, meat, and vegetables onto a wide knife and lift them to his mouth. He sometimes used mashed potatoes to stabilize pesky peas that might roll off.

Harman's daughter-in-law Emma, my grandmother, was a conservative farm wife but not immune to modern times. She had some modern, narrower table knives like most people use now. Maybe they had been a gift. One day she set the table with the new silverware, including the new-style knives, not thinking of her widowed father-in-law Harman, who was coming for supper.

The food was tasty, nourishing, and fortified with salt, pepper, butter, sugar, and lard. All was well until Harman tried to balance a few peas on the narrow table knife. He tried once, and the peas rolled off. He tried again, and they rolled off again. He was especially careful the third time, but the peas rolled right off *again*. That was too much, *way* too much.

"Dot knife iss not goot forr eating!" he roared and threw the knife across the kitchen.

Emma quickly brought out one of the old knives, and peace returned to the peas.

From then on, Harman's pronouncement on the new knife was often quoted, always out of his hearing: "Dot knife iss not goot forr eating!"

20
Harman's Third Wife

HARMAN KARDATZKE WAS MARRIED three times. His first wife was my great-grandmother, Henriette Wilhelmine Marie Smith (1864–1926). She gave birth to my grandfather Fred, his four sisters, and his brother Tony. Fred and his wife Emma gave birth to my father, Arlin, and his eight siblings. I was born in 1939. If you do the arithmetic, you'll realize that I never met Henriette (or Henrietta) before she died.

Sometime after Henriette's death, Harman had a brief marriage to a woman whose name has disappeared from memory and written records. To be fair, she may not have been the floozy that some have suspected. She may have been an attractive, sensible, intelligent Christian woman. Maybe Harman had been smitten when he met her but was soon cured of his love sickness. Or maybe Harman was too large a mission project for the good lady. For whatever reason, the marriage ended quickly.

After the embers of that marriage cooled, Harman married a widow named Mrs. Sherk. My ancestry research has not surrendered up her first name. She is known to me only as Mrs. Sherk. In fact, that's exactly what my great-grandfather called her.

Imagine Harman coming in from field work and asking, "Vott's forr supper, Mrs. Sherk?" Or imagine her after supper as she was handing him a piece of pie for dessert hearing, "Can I haff some coffee, too, Mrs. Sherk?"

I once told someone about Harman calling his third wife Mrs. Sherk. The person asked, "Was it a joke?"

"No, Harman was not a joker."

"Was he being harsh?"

"No, he just always called her Mrs. Sherk."

"Then why did he call her that?"

All I can imagine is that their relationship as man and wife, coming late in life after previous marriages, called for a certain dignity, even formality. It was probably a marriage for companionship, maybe just a marriage of convenience. Both were common in those days. Or maybe Harman had known her previous husband and held him in such high esteem that he felt he couldn't be on a first-name basis with the man's widow.

After Mrs. Sherk's passing, Harman lived his remaining years alone as a so-called "widower" (a widow-man) before he died in 1941. If others in the family knew more about Mrs. Sherk than what's here, they chose not to share it with me. Now you know all I know about her.

Rest in peace, Harman and Mrs. Sherk.

Harman with Henrietta, the woman who partly tamed him.

21
Planting Trees for Posterity

Late in Harman Kardatzke's life, during the Depression of the 1930s, he worked planting trees in Harris Township, the home region of Elmore, Ohio. He was in his seventies, so planting small trees might have been all he could handle. Among the trees that Harman planted are the ones on the south side of Route 105 just east of US Route 51. Those maple trees, still there, have been mature trees for a long time.

Why did Harman plant trees? Maybe he earned a little money from the farmer who owned the land and was selling residential lots. Maybe the highway department paid him. Maybe he was part of a Depression recovery program sponsored by President Franklin Roosevelt, who was willing to try anything to put men back to work.

The truth is no one knows why Harman planted the trees. The few who have ever heard of Harman Kardatzke, now including the readers of this story, can choose to look at the trees and picture a hardened old Prussian, softened a little by age, showing a kinder, gentler side of himself, even if he did do it for pay.

22
Harman's Purloined Overcoat

DAMSCHRODER'S STORE IN ELMORE had a long history. The store was operating in 1865 under the original owner, so it probably had opened some years earlier. It was a trusted store that lived by the motto "What you buy we stand by."

In the late 1800s and early 1900s, Damschroder's was a general store where people could buy almost anything from groceries and clothing to tools and laundry soap. In its later years in the 1970s, the ladies who ran it mainly sold clothing, but they also sold toys, some of them quite old. In those later years, the store still had the old bins where in earlier times customers might have bought scoops of cornmeal, sugar, or flour. The general store closed in the 1970s and was reopened later as an antiques store.

On a visit to the antique store in the 1990s, the owner took me to the attic to show me an old receipt that seemed to tell a story. It was a receipt for an overcoat the store had sold to Harman Kardatzke in 1910. Harman had signed for the coat but had never paid for it. The man who owned the antique store didn't expect me to pay for the coat; he just thought I would be interested. I was, in fact, very interested. I knew the story of the coat and the receipt, and I told the shopkeeper an abbreviated version of the story.

Imagine a young man taking shelter in Damschroder's just as an early winter storm was breaking. "I'd like to buy a coat," he may have announced.

"Let me show you our winter coats," the clerk would have replied politely, leading the way to the back of the store. "Will this be for farm work or for Sunday best?"

"Sunday best."

The coat might have been among the gray and black tweeds, common then, and it would be like armor against the cold winter wind outside.

"I'll take this one," the young man would have said.

"Fine choice, sir. Please come up here and I'll write up a ticket for it," the clerk would have replied and led the man to the front desk, where he would have jotted the date and the coat's description on a receipt. "And how will you pay for it, sir?" he'd have asked, expecting an answer of cash or a promise of a future payment.

"Just put it on my bill. I'll come back in a few days to pay for it."

"Fine, fine! And what is your name, if I may ask?"

"Harmon Kardatzke."

"Oh, yes, fine, Mr. Kardatzke." The clerk certainly would have heard of Harman Kardatzke and his farm on Graytown Road. The clerk must have assumed this young man was a son of the farmer. After entering "Harman Kardatzke" on the receipt, he would have placed it in his register for safekeeping.

Off went the young man in his new winter coat, and he was never seen again in Elmore.

A few weeks later, local farm owner Harman Kardatzke walked into Damschroder's store looking for a pair of gloves and a winter hat. He was forty-eight years old then and had the confident air of a Prussian farmer. Choosing a pair of gloves and a hat that fit his status in life, he went to the counter to pay.

"Will you also be paying for the winter coat now as well, Mr. Kardatzke?" the clerk asked politely.

Harman's head jerked up, and he glared at the clerk. "Und vott coat might dot be?" he demanded.

"Oh! Don't you remember? The coat from a few weeks ago."

"I don't forget!" he grumbled, "Und I didn't buy no new coat."

"Oh! I'm sorry! I didn't make the sale, but I know we are carrying the bill for a coat. It was signed by Harman Kardatzke."

"Dot vasn't me. Maybe you got the wrong name."

"Here, Mr. Kardatzke, I'll show you the bill."

The clerk's hands began to shake as he searched the drawer for the receipt. "Here it is. See, right here is where it was signed: Harmon Kardatzke."

"Dott's not me!" Harman thundered.

It all came clear. Harman's ne'er-do-well nephew Harmon (spelled with an "o") had taken the coat and signed for it, not knowing the difference in spelling between his name and his uncle's, nor did the salesperson know. Harman had not seen Harmon for several years, but he knew his nephew's reputation for dishonesty and devious tricks.

Harman burned with anger, but he wouldn't let the store have this claim against his family and his good reputation, and not even against his wayward nephew who carried the Kardatzke name. Harman went to the Bank of Elmore and withdrew enough cash to pay for the coat.

"Ven dott nepew off mine comes back, you keep him *right here*," Harman said menacingly thumping the counter with his massive index finger. "Den I vill come und *settle* vit him."

The clerk nodded nervously, and Harman stomped out.

The end of the story has been lost in the mists of the Great Black Swamp. Perhaps Harman visited his brother Henry, the father of young Harmon. Perhaps the matter was settled in a friendly, brotherly way. Or a bitter argument may have erupted. At least no shooting or other violence made its way into the papers.

(Henry Kardatzke was the blackest of the black sheep of the family. An elderly aunt told me that Henry killed his wife, tried to kill young Harmon, and escaped to Africa and died there. Rumor had it that he found a gold mine in Africa before his demise. No Kardatzke ever tried to cash in on the gold mine.)

"Burn this Letter"

Under Harman Kardatzke's own roof, romance was brewing in 1901. His teenage daughter, Minnie, was being courted by a farm boy who had a flair for letter writing. The boy wisely intended the letter to be for Minnie's eyes only, keeping it secret from her strict Prussian father. At the end of his passionate letter he wrote, "Burn this up." Minnie did not burn the letter but slid it through a crack in her bedroom wall, and there it remained for decades.

Harman's house, where Minnie grew up, later passed to Minnie's brother Frederick, and it was later sold outside the family. Workers found the letter inside a wall at the home in the 1980s. They had opened the wall for a remodeling project, and they found the 1901 love letter was where it had been for over eighty years. The homeowner gave the letter to Arlin Kardatzke and it entered family lore.

Minnie was born in 1887, and John Langerman was born in 1881. She was fourteen and he was twenty when he wrote to her, so he had ample reason to fear Harman's wrath. She was eighteen when they married in 1905 and he was twenty-four.

John wrote the letter in a single column in a staggered layout. It is reproduced here preserving most of the original spelling and punctuation. John probably had ridden a horse to Minnie's home the night before he wrote the letter. He reports that he reached home at nearly 1:00 a.m.

If you think there was no romantic passion in the early 1900s, read this letter and blush. John and Minnie probably will smile to see that their secret finally has been made so public after so long.

Leatherport, Ohio

Elmore Ohio Oct 28th 1901

My Dear Friend,

I thought I would better write to you this noon so you will get it soon. I sppose you are waiting for a letter from me. I thought I would better write to my Pet or you might get lone-some. Well Pet I got home allright last night it was about one oclock I got plenty of sleep last night I hope you did to.

I awoke about six oclock this morning and I was more than lone-some for you Pet. I husked corn all fore noon it was pretty good husking

Well I will half to close now Pet. So good-bye Pet my Dear Pet good-bye. I send my best regards to you and ooooooooooo kisses to you Pet and all my love and a good many sweet wishes to you Pet so good-bye Pet my sweet Darling Pet good-bye.

From your loveing friend
John Langermann. answer soon.

Burn this up.

Part Five

Pond and Lake Stories

23
The Gleckler Ponds

———�֍———

THE PONDS ON GRAYTOWN ROAD were more novel in the 1940s than today since ponds now line the Ohio Turnpike where their soil was borrowed for nearby overpasses. In the utterly flat land of the former Great Black Swamp, farmers were determined to rid the area of standing water and make the land arable for farming. Christopher Gleckler and his son George had a reason to gouge the rich farmland for the valuable clay beneath, and they created new ponds in the process. Happily, the ponds were dry in the warm months when the tile yard was operating, thanks to the pond-draining pump described earlier.

Today, besides mosquitoes, the fields and streams around Leatherport are home to pheasants, ducks, deer, raccoons, opossums, rabbits, muskrats, weasels, turtles, frogs, snakes, birds, fish, clams, bats, skunks, mice, rats, and dew worms. Migrating Canada geese rest and feed in cornfields near the ponds in the fall. The most dangerous wild animals now are the deer that can suddenly pop up in front of a passing car. A raccoon can be dangerous if cornered in a barn or caught in a trap, and bats can carry rabies. Otherwise, nearly all the wild animals are now game for hunters or novelties to report to the Department of Natural Resources (DNR).

Because of the Gleckler ponds, there was plenty to do in all seasons of the year in Leatherport in the mid-1900s. The ponds offered swimming, fishing, skating, and frog hunting, besides sighting migrating wildlife that stopped in at various seasons. Tall herons stalked the big pond in summer, terrorizing small fish. Muskrats undermined the shores of the ponds, and they built cattail dens in the biggest pond. Raccoons hunted for the slimy things they like to eat. Stinky skunks made themselves known from time to time around the ponds or when they were squashed flat on the road. Red-winged blackbirds built nests in the cattails. Snakes slithered through the grass near the ponds, and turtles laid eggs in lawns and fields. Owls hooted their eerie message in barns at night.

The moods of the ponds changed with the seasons. Waves on the big pond made it seem like an ocean to young kids, and the smell of dead fish and seaweed helped our imaginations. Wind, rain, snow, and cold weather all played their parts. In summer, the pond water was warm and good for swimming and fishing. Fish liked summer, too, and they were easy to catch. Turtles especially liked summer, the time when they would bask in the sun for hours on any flat place next to the pond. In autumn the turtles and snakes began to disappear into their winter quarters, and a ghostly haze hung over the ponds on the first cold mornings.

The first thin layer of glass-like ice signaled the beginning of winter and the skating season. When spring warming started, the thick winter ice melted first in the shallows next to the shore and created a water moat that kept most late-spring skaters at bay. Avid skaters like my father sometimes jumped the moat or brought a plank as a bridge over the moat to the solid ice. A rite of spring each year was my father's last wet foot from a leap to the ice.

No bears or wolves roamed Leatherport in the 1940s and 1950s as they did in the early 1800s, so we kids had to invent them if we wanted any.

Deer reappeared near Leatherport in the late twentieth century. Now they sometimes dare motorists to run them over. Bears and wolves have yet to return, but the future of the Leatherport area has not yet been written.

The ponds spawned many stories. The best ones I know follow here.

24
The Playground Canvas

THE FLAT LAND AROUND LEATHERPORT was like a blank canvas on which pictures of fun and play could be drawn. Some of the fun at Leatherport was natural, and some was man-made. Arlin Kardatzke, my father, was born in Leatherport and lived there nearly all his life. He had a special affection for the place as a child and much later as an old man. Skating was a favorite activity for him. He became an expert skater in his childhood and continued to skate on his pond until he was eighty-two years old.

Arlin created most of the man-made fun. He was famous for the amusements he created for his children and the neighborhood kids. We kids always had several swings. Some hung from limbs over the lawn, but some sent us soaring over the pond or over the deep ditch beside the road. One swing hung from especially high on a cable over the pond, so we could drop from the swing into the pond halfway to the middle.

Soon after my family moved to the pond house in 1943, my dad built a zip line between two of the big maple trees in the former Leatherport School yard. A swing seat hung below a pulley on the zip line cable. As a Sun Oil employee, Arlin was able to salvage the cable for free from the Toledo refinery. The cable was half an inch in diameter and was strong enough to suspend a full-size car, something we never did but knew as possible. The zip line became the most dramatic and popular of all the rides my dad created. We called the zip line a "trolley" because we didn't really know what a trolley was. We kids were still living in "the olden days" when zip lines were unknown.

The merry-go-round my father built was another favorite of all the kids around and many grown-ups. It went faster than any other playground merry-go-round. To build it, he got the rear axle from an old truck and took apart the differential gear so only one wheel would turn when the drive shaft turned. He took off one of the wheels and put that end of the axle in a big hole in the ground with the other end up in the air with the wheel and tire still attached. He poured cement in the hole, stood the axle perfectly straight up in it, and steadied the axel so that it would remain perfectly upright overnight. When the cement had dried into solid concrete, he put a long, sturdy plank across the top of the tire and bolted it on. He hung a swing seat at each end of the board.

To make the merry-go-round turn, he attached a steering wheel to where the driveshaft entered the axle. Turning the steering wheel made the tire and board and the two swings whirl around. A big kid or a grown-up could turn the steering wheel to make the two swings go around faster and faster. At top speed, the kids in the swings would be flying nearly straight out. It was never good to get in the way of the flying riders.

Among the natural play choices, we kids especially loved to fish in the ponds. Sometimes the sunfish were so hungry they would jump out of the water to bite an empty hook. To catch the larger bullheads, we used worms that we dug up in the garden, but sometimes we went hunting at night for "dew worms." On warm, humid nights, these huge worms slithered up from their underground homes to lie out on the grass. It was as though they were sunbathing at night, which could only make sense to a dew worm. We could sneak up on the worms quietly with flashlights and grab them before they could slide back into their holes. To the fish, they were delicious. We never tasted the worms ourselves.

All summer we could hear a chorus of frogs singing at night around the ponds. Their voices ranged from little soprano chirps to the ponderous, deep bass voices of the bullfrogs. One of my uncles made a tape recording of the frog choir on an especially tuneful night, and he pretended to lead the choir by instructions he included in the recording. He gave his directions to the frogs in English, and they responded as he asked. They were smart frogs, he said.

At least once or twice each summer, we went frog hunting. We needed a flashlight and a bag, and we might have a frog spear or a BB gun. Sometimes we could catch a big frog just by shining a light on it and getting close enough to grab it. Once we kids caught so many frogs that Mama cooked the frog legs for breakfast the next morning. Stand-up comics joke that a food "tastes like chicken." Frog legs *do* taste like chicken.

We hunted by daylight, too, mostly rabbits and pheasants in the fall. As a teenager, I shot a couple of rabbits and skinned them for cooking. I never succeeded in shooting a pheasant, but I did shoot in the general direction of a pheasant once. I was walking along the edge of a field of standing corn, hoping to see a pheasant and get off a good shot. Suddenly a beautiful cock pheasant flew up thirty feet in front of me. By the time I clicked off the safety and raised the shotgun, the pheasant was safely out of range. I pulled the trigger, but my shot went wild. The pheasant lived to startle another hunter some other day.

As young trappers, we tried to catch muskrats, and we sometimes succeeded. Their dark brown pelts were valued for fur coats and gloves, and it wasn't hard to figure out where the muskrats were. They usually lived in tunnels around the edges of the large pond. We could set a trap underwater in a tunnel and catch a muskrat in a day or two. Since muskrats could damage cornfields and garden crops, we felt justified in trapping them; but we might have trapped them anyway, even if they had been living on snakes and bugs and minding their own business.

Some farm boys made money trapping muskrats and other furry animals. After catching and killing an animal, they had to skin it and dry the pelt so it could be mailed to Sears, Roebuck and Company. It was grim work, and the money was hardly worth it, but there was a feeling of primitive adventure in trapping. If we had cared more about history, we could have pretended we were early French fur trappers, but we weren't that well educated.

For most of the summer, we kids went barefoot. As soon as school was out, my brothers and I would put our shoes away and only pull them out for church on Sundays all summer. Our feet were tender on Memorial Day but tough by Labor Day. It was hard to walk across our gravel driveway in bare feet when school was first out for the summer, but by the end of summer, our feet had such thick calluses that we could run on stones and not get hurt.

On the first hot days of summer, all the kids in our neighborhood got sunburns, mostly from swimming in the pond. Peeling off our sunburned skin was one of the main rites of summer, especially if we were burned severely enough to raise blisters and cause our skin to peel. We once formed a circle in the lawn and peeled each other's backs in celebration of summer.

Summer was a time when the grass was green, the water was clear and blue, and the white limestone road gleamed as brightly as a Greek temple. We kids grew especially fast then. None of us looked the same when we went back to school after summer vacation. Everyone was taller, tanned, and wiser after what we had done in the summer.

25
Turtle King

TWO KINDS OF TURTLES LIVED IN the pond next to our house: snapping turtles and painted turtles. The painted turtles lived a happy, peaceful life until the summer when I became Turtle King.

On hot summer days, the painted turtles went swimming and sunned themselves on the trunks of a large cottonwood tree that had blown over into the pond. Painted turtles' shells were shiny brown like Ohio's famous buckeyes. Their underbellies were like a kaleidoscope of yellow and red geometric tiles. Snapping turtles were thorny and ugly and they skulked in the pond-bottom muck. They looked prehistoric and were said to be able to hold your finger in their knife-like jaws until sundown if one caught you. Even if you cut off a snapping turtle's head, we believed the beast would not let go.

Painted turtles took long morning and afternoon naps with happy dreams of bugs and fish they could catch for supper. They could bite, but we kids avoided being bitten by simply holding them with a hand stretched across the top of their shiny backs.

I wasn't Turtle King when summer started that year. I earned the title by catching more turtles than anyone before or since. Mama was the first to call me the "Turtle King," and it made me feel important and skilled and powerful. I may have been seven or nine years old. I know because I couldn't have been eight when I was the Turtle King because that was the year my father and Earl Sandrock drained the pond. The turtles went into hiding that year in the small pond behind the icehouse. We kids never fished or caught frogs in that pond, so the turtles were safe.

There were two main ways we caught painted turtles. One way was with a garden rake, the kind with strong pointed teeth that point straight down. If a sunning turtle saw us coming and swam under the moss, we could sometimes catch him by raking the moss to shore, turtle and all. We could drag the turtle back toward us, along with some moss or weeds the turtle was trying to hide in, and grab it by reaching across its back to hold it on its sides before it could scamper back into the pond.

The other way we caught painted turtles was from a boat. When we first moved to the pond house, my father built a plywood boat in the shape of a barge. It had a flat bottom and vertical sides, and it was about twelve feet long. The sides were about a foot tall. The boat curved up at both ends, so we could row it backward as well as forward. It floated so high in the water that it was easy to row, which was good for the small kids we were. The plywood boat just skimmed over the surface of the pond unless a big gang of kids got in and weighed it down. It had a narrow deck at the front and back, and a kid could lie across either deck to reach down into the water and grab a turtle.

When I used the boat alone, I discovered that the best way to catch a turtle was to watch the surface of the pond until one poked its head up. I would row the boat slowly toward it and, at just the right moment, I would run to the front of the boat and fling myself over the little deck. From there I could plunge both hands down to the place where I had seen the turtle, grab it, and bring it into the boat.

All summer long I caught painted turtles. I kept them in a pen in shallow water at the edge of the pond, and soon I had eight or ten of them. Somehow, I also caught four medium-size snapping turtles and put them in a big bucket separate from the painted turtles.

With all this wealth in turtles, I decided to go into business. I found a wooden shingle and a small can of white paint in the garage, and I painted this sign:

Turtles for Sale, 50 cents each

Snapping Turtles Free

I put the sign and the bucket of turtles out by our gravel road where cars and trucks and tractors went by, a few each day. I kept watching the bucket while I worked at catching more turtles, but no one stopped. The road in front of the house wasn't busy that day or any day. Only about eight cars went past all afternoon, and none of them stopped.

When it was nearly suppertime, Mama came out to see what I was doing. She had seen the bucket out by the road and wondered what it was for. I proudly showed her the snapping turtles and told her about my plan to sell the painted turtles.

"I think you better put the snapping turtles back in the pond," she advised me. "Most people don't know how to handle snapping turtles, and these seem to be suffering from the heat in that bucket."

I was getting tired of operating my business, so I took my mother's advice and started toward the pond with the bucket of turtles. Mama had seen the cage by the pond where I kept the painted turtles before, and she thought about it a minute.

"I wonder if you should turn the other turtles loose too," she said. "You'll be going back to school next week, and you won't be able to take care of them anymore. Maybe you should let them get bigger so you can catch them next summer. You might be Turtle King again next year."

That made sense. Besides, it was hot, and I was getting tired of my responsibilities as Turtle King. I dumped the snapping turtles into the pond and looked at my beautiful collection of painted turtles. They ignored me, of course. Turtles aren't very sociable. I lifted the edge of the cage, and the painted turtles paddled frantically to get out into open water and hide under moss.

The turtles were mostly safe for the rest of the warm weather that year, though I did catch a couple of them again just to show my great power as Turtle King. I had never had such luck hunting anything before, and I was only seven years old or maybe nine. I had a great future.

I never became Turtle King again. By the next summer, I had outgrown that goal. When people asked me if I was catching turtles again, I just shook my head. I was too mature for that. I don't know what I did that summer, but it was surely nothing as important as being Turtle King. I was never a king of any kind again.

26
Joe the Turtle

⸎

ONE OF THE TURTLES I CAUGHT the year I was Turtle King was an unusually large painted turtle. His armor-plated back was nicely mounded, and his tummy was especially pretty. I put him in a bucket in the garage to look at for a few days.

Finally, my mother said, "Don't you think you should let that turtle go? He can't catch any food in that bucket in the garage. Maybe you should put him back in the pond."

I knew she was right, but I didn't want to lose my friendship with the turtle. I had already named him Joe. (I didn't know if he was a boy turtle or a girl turtle, but that didn't matter.) If I put Joe back in the pond, I might not be able to tell him from other turtles.

Why not label him? I thought.

There was still some white paint in the can I had used when I painted my "Turtles for Sale" sign. "Perfect! I'll paint 'Joe' on Joe's back, and I'll be able to see him all summer long."

I found a paintbrush small enough for writing, and I painted "Joe" on Joe's back as carefully as I could. It was lucky I had named him "Joe" and not a longer name like "Willard" or "Robert." A longer name might not have fit on his back. I let the paint dry for an hour or two, and then I carried Joe to the pond and gently set him down in the shallow water. Joe didn't stop and think long. He paddled right out into the pond and dived down so deep I couldn't see him.

"Goodbye, Joe," I said.

When he was far enough from shore to feel safe, he stuck his head above the water. I'm not sure he actually looked directly at me, his friend. He just looked around. I couldn't tell from the expression on his face how he felt about being in the pond again, but I think he was happy. Then he ducked under again, and he stayed down so long I had to leave.

Summer turned to fall, and fall turned to winter, and the weather became cold. At first, ice formed only in the grass at the pond's edge where the water splashed up and froze in the cold night air. A week or two later, a night came when it was much colder. The next morning, a sheet of glass seemed to cover the pond. That first thin sheet of ice was especially beautiful. Like a mirror, it reflected the blue sky on clear days. Like a window, it showed the leaves and sticks on the bottom of the pond. You could look down into the pond and imagine being a tiny submarine cruising around down there.

In a few more days, snow fell and made the pond a smooth, bright, flat place. We kids could walk in circles and make designs on it. When the snow wasn't too deep, we could scrape it off and go skating. In all those times, I never thought of Joe.

As the winter went on, the ice sometimes melted and then froze again. Sometimes so much snow came and piled up so deep that even my father couldn't shovel it off for skating, and he loved skating.

That winter there was snow on the ice until it all melted in a January warm spell. Then the air became very cold and the air was calm. Beautiful, clear ice reformed on the pond, and no snow came to cover it. Night after night the temperature went below zero, and the ice thickened. Soon the ice was thick enough to hold up young boys and girls. It must have been three inches thick, and it was so smooth and clear that I could look right through the ice to the bottom of the pond.

One morning I lay down on the ice and held my hands at the sides of my face to see to the bottom of the pond. Then I saw him! There was Joe the Turtle! The white letters I had painted on his back made him easy to see. "J-O-E" the letters said. It was Joe for sure. I was happy I had painted his name on him.

"There's Joe!" I yelled.

The other kids came and looked and yelled. "It's Joe the Turtle! Come and look!"

Then one kid said, "I think he's dead. He's not swimming."

We all looked again, and it was true. Joe wasn't swimming to get away, even with us kids standing right above him on the clear ice, talking and yelling.

"He can't be dead!" I yelled, almost crying. "Maybe he drowned but can come alive again," I said hopefully.

Another kid said, "Maybe he's just cold. Maybe he'll be okay if we can take him in the house to warm up." This made sense. We knew how our fingers and toes felt numb when they were cold.

"Get a hatchet! Chop a hole in the ice!" a boy yelled.

I ran to the garage and got the hatchet. I chopped at the ice. Chips flew in all directions as I hacked open a hole big enough for Joe to pass through. Another kid ran to the garage for a hoe so we could lift Joe out.

I pushed the hoe down and gently slipped the blade under Joe. He slowly came to the surface on the hoe. When Joe was on top of the open water, I set him down on the ice for all the kids to see.

"It's Joe for sure," said a neighbor kid. "There's his name."

"Is he dead?" a small girl asked.

"No! He's not dead," a bigger, older girl said. "He's hibernating."

"Hibernating" was not a word that all the kids knew.

"Does that mean he's sleeping?" a younger kid asked.

"Something like that," the bigger girl said calmly. She seemed to know a lot about turtles and hibernation.

I didn't really know what "hibernating" meant, but I didn't think it was good for Joe to be under the ice in that cold water. If he hadn't drowned, he did seem to be almost frozen. He didn't move, and I felt sure he would like to warm up.

"I'm taking him in the house to warm him up," I announced.

I picked Joe up, and none of the other kids tried to stop me. They knew Joe was my friend. Besides, they didn't want to touch a wet, cold turtle. Back in the house, I found a cardboard box just the right size for Joe to sleep in. I put Joe in his box behind our stove and made sure there was enough coal to keep the stove burning the rest of the afternoon.

About bedtime, I checked on Joe. He was moving! He was trying to crawl. Or maybe he was still sleeping and was having a dream of swimming in the pond. I felt so happy! I had saved Joe's life by bringing him in to warm up. At bedtime I went upstairs to bed with my brothers, and I slept well, knowing that Joe was sleeping safely downstairs.

The next morning before breakfast, I checked on Joe. He was sleeping again, probably from being up so late the night before, I thought. My brothers and I had our corn flakes, put on our warm coats, and went out to the road to wait for the school bus.

When the bus brought us home that afternoon, I was the first one in the house. I ran straight to Joe. He was still in his box, but my mother had moved him away from the stove. Joe was still sleeping.

"Did Joe wake up while I was at school?" I asked my mother.

"No, he's been like that all day. I checked on him several times, and he always looked like that," she said.

"Do you think he will wake up tomorrow morning?" I asked.

My mother sat down on a chair to talk to me. "I don't know if Joe will ever wake up," she said. "Turtles spend the whole winter in the pond when it's frozen. They hibernate under the ice."

Hibernate. There was that word again. I didn't say anything, so she continued.

"Turtles warm up slowly when the ice melts and the pond gets warmer," she said. "I think Joe may have woken up too fast. He may not be able to wake up again."

Then I felt sad. Joe might not wake up. The warm house wasn't good for him. We wouldn't be able to see him next summer with "Joe" on his back if he didn't wake up.

My mother knew I felt sad. "If he doesn't wake up by morning, I'll ask Daddy to find a place for him outside," my mother said. "Then if he wakes up, he can find a place to hide."

I felt better. There were lots of places to hide outside, and maybe Joe would go to one of them when he got cold enough to wake up again.

My dad found a place for him outside, but I never asked where that place was, and we never saw Joe again. I don't know if Joe ever did wake up.

The next summer, we kids caught other turtles, and we painted names on two of them with white paint. We saw them several times that summer, and once we saw one of them under the ice the next winter, but we didn't chop a hole and pull him out. We remembered what had happened to Joe.

27
Lake Erie

---◆---

NOT FAR FROM LEATHERPORT, the shimmering beauty of Lake Erie beckoned my family every year. A highlight of the summer was a short trip to one of the Lake Erie beaches, and the nearest was only ten miles from Leatherport. As simple folk, swimming was the only thing we did at Lake Erie. We didn't fish there in the summer or winter. We didn't go ice fishing on the lake in winter. We didn't take our huge, luxurious sailboat there in summer either. We didn't even *have* a huge, luxurious sailboat. We had only the pond boat that Daddy had built. But we did take inner tubes to float on in Lake Erie.

There was a feeling of romance about Lake Erie. Just knowing that the Canadian border ran through the middle of the lake was exciting. Actual soil of Canada was fairly close, and we could listen to CKLW radio broadcasts from Windsor, Canada, just across the lake.

A ferryboat sailed from the town of Port Clinton to Put-in-Bay Island and gave us a sample of oceanic travel. We could almost lose sight of shore on the trip, and that was a thrill. Perry's Monument on the island celebrated the American victory over the British in a battle nearby in the War of 1812. We kids cared nothing about that war. We just wanted the elevator ride to the top of the monument so we could look down on the ant-like creatures below who happened to be people.

Swimming in Lake Erie in those days was heavenly. We bobbed around on gentle waves and found clam and snail shells along the shore. The water was so nutritiously green that we could almost drink it, and sometimes we did gulp some lake water down by accident.

Then came the pollution of the 1960s. Fish died by the millions, and their bodies washed up on sandy beaches. Curious kids looked at the dead fish, but their parents found them revolting. The lake was like a cesspool, and people no longer went there to swim. Something had to be done to save the lake, and it was, in fact, saved by a major cleanup and pollution control.

Today Lake Erie is back to its former health, if not better. Swimming is popular again now, and the lake has become one of the best places in the world to fish for walleye, one of the most delicious fish for humans to eat.

Arlin and Ruth Kardatzke in Lake Erie in 1935 when its water was pure.

28
Over Lake Erie in a Three-Engine Plane

AFTER WORLD WAR II, MY FATHER would have liked to be a pilot and fly for fun or maybe for income. He even took a few flying lessons, but the expense of lessons and the needs of his growing family put a stop to his ambition for flight. He never stopped dreaming about flying though.

Sometime in the 1950s, the company that operated flights to Put-in-Bay and other Lake Erie Islands announced cheap rides on one of their Ford Tri-Motor planes. My dad heard the news.

"How about we take a ride?" he asked me.

"Sure!" I said eagerly.

I don't know why my dad asked me and none of my brothers or sisters. Maybe he did ask them, and they didn't want to go. Maybe the idea of flying out over the lake in an ancient airplane seemed life-threatening to them. Whatever the reason, I was glad to go.

Ford Tri-motor over the corncrib and barn
at the Kardatzke farm on Graytown Road.

Over Lake Erie in a Three-Engine Plane

My only previous flight had been in 1949 in my Uncle Paul's Piper Cub for a circuit around my grandfather's farm on Graytown Road. By then I was nine years old. This flight to Put-in-Bay would be in a much larger plane and would go out over the lake. If it veered far enough over the lake to reach Canada, I thought, it would be an international flight! I was fifteen and ready for international travel, but only that much of it.

My memory is hazy about where our flight took off and landed. It might have been at Port Clinton, right on Lake Erie, or it might have been at the Toledo airport or maybe even at "Haar Field," a grass landing strip near Elmore operated by a farmer named Paul Haar. But my memory of the plane is clear. It was huge, bigger than I expected, and its sides appeared to be made of corrugated steel. To me it looked like a flying granary for storing wheat like the ones I had seen on farms around Leatherport, but it must have had a skin of aluminum for lighter weight.

On each wing was a large rotary engine with pistons protruding all around. A big wooden propeller was at the front of each engine. The third engine was mounted at the plane's nose in front of the two pilots. That engine looked like the other two engines except for its odd location. It was designed to give the plane a better chance of survival if one of the other two engines stopped. It was an extra engine, for safety purposes, and it wasn't a bad idea in a time when flying was more dangerous than now. It must have worked; the Ford Tri-Motor was an especially reliable and safe airplane.

When my father and I boarded the plane, the experience was a little like entering a barn. The seats were hard and basic, just one row of benches on each side of the plane facing the center. Other inexperienced passengers entered after us, took seats, and joked nervously about the perils of flying. All of us buckled in for takeoff. If there was an announcement about flight safety and what to do if we went down in the lake, I didn't hear it.

A sound like an explosion outside the plane let us know the engines were starting. The noise rose, and the whole plane shook. All three engines came to life with a deafening roar, and the plane shook, eager for takeoff. A few minutes later, the plane trundled onto the runway, and we were airborne at about 65 miles per hour.

Leatherport, Ohio

Land and trees slipped under us, and we were soon over Lake Erie, probably no more than 2,000 feet above the gentle waves. We probably reached a top speed of 100 miles per hour, the plane's usual cruising speed. In a few minutes, Put-in-Bay Island was under us. We circled the island and saw Perry's Monument, and we headed back for the mainland without arousing any Canadians' fears on their side of the lake.

My dad was grinning with pleasure the whole time, and he tried to point out interesting mechanical features inside the plane. I learned next to nothing: The roar of the mighty piston engines drowned out thought as well as speech. The next thing we knew we were making a soft but bouncing landing. Some of the farmers on the plane joked nervously and looked relieved to step out of our flying granary onto solid land.

"How about that?" my dad asked over the ringing in my ears. "We flew over the lake!"

I nodded and tucked away the memory of our flight. I was a Future Farmer of America, and I was as happy as my fellow farmers to be on the ground again.

I didn't realize how historic our flight was. We had flown in one of the pioneer aircraft of the twentieth century. A few Ford Tri-Motor planes still exist, and some are even airworthy. I'm glad we rode in that ancient plane when we had a chance.

(The Ford Tri-Motor was nicknamed "The Tin Goose," an allusion to the "Tin Lizzie" nickname for one of Henry Ford's early car models.)

Part Six

Farm Stories

29
Family Farms

---·❉·---

I WAS BORN IN THE VILLAGE OF Lindsey, Ohio, in 1939, just in time to see old-style family farming before it changed radically after World War II. In 1945, self-sufficient family farms still produced food for home consumption as well as for the local and national markets. Most farms raised chickens, hogs, beef steers, and dairy cows. A few outliers raised sheep, goats, ducks, or geese. Nearly every farm had an apple orchard and a few peach, pear, plum, and apricot trees. Many had vineyards for table grapes and sometimes for wine.

Families were large then because farm work called for many hands. Families of nine or more children were common. Every member of the family worked on the family farm, and most farmers hoped to pass their farms on to their children as an inheritance.

Farms around Leatherport were mostly manual operations before World War II, though tractors and other machinery had been invading for several decades. By 1950, major changes were transforming the farming world in America. Mechanized, specialized farming was taking over. Huge tractors, self-propelled combines, and milking machines appeared. The quaint "chores" that dominated family farm life were transformed or eliminated by machinery.

By 1960, little remained of the family farms where my grandparents had lived and worked. The land was there, and so were the houses and outbuildings, but there was very little of the prewar manual labor. Farms were becoming businesses, sometimes operating on a large industrial scale. Thankfully, I was born early enough to see the traditional family farming way of life before it vanished.

A glimpse of old-time farming.

30
Farm Auctions – the End and New Beginnings

———✤———

THE BEGINNING AND END OF MANY farms was an auction. One home's ending was the beginning of another. The furniture, quilts, lamps, dishes, pots and pans from one household were used and treasured by someone else's new household. Land, farm machinery, and livestock were usually part of a farm auction, but the most colorful auctions involved the personal belongings from people's homes.

People went to auctions early in their marriages when they were setting up housekeeping, and much later they held auctions when the household was being broken up by a death or declining family fortunes. Emotions were never more mingled than in household auctions where treasured objects of a lifetime were auctioned to impersonal crowds. The objects told stories how the people lived, how they cooked, what dishes held their food, and what the people themselves wore next to their bodies while they were living.

The words "While they were living" were part of many auction scenes. In some cases, a farmer died, and his widow needed money from the auction to sustain her for the remaining days of her life. She sold what she couldn't take to her next home, usually a smaller place, and her deceased husband's clothes often were auctioned off with the housewares. His straight razors, shaving mugs, razor strop, and wide suspenders went with the clothes.

Leatherport auctions had what I imagined as the aura the Old World. We didn't have peasants around Leatherport to add local color, but we had farmers and their wives, townspeople, kids, and old folks, many of whom came only for the entertainment of an auction. If you arrived after an auction had started, you would find a sizeable crowd gathered around a man standing slighting taller than the others. In front of him and behind him were tables of household objects, and furniture dotted the lawn or filled a porch.

As you approached the crowd, you could hear the mesmerizing cadence of the auctioneer. The rhythmic chanting of numbers and urgings to buy drew people in, sometimes against their will. Sometimes things were sold for "pennies on the dollar." Sometimes competitive bidding drove the price of a chair or lamp up beyond reason. Sometimes there were "shills," or fake bidders, planted in the crowd to drive the bidding. The auctioneer's chatter remains vivid in my memory.

"Now we have this lovely lamp. Who'll be the lucky one to buy it? What'll you pay? Let's start it off at a dollar. Who'll make it a dollar?"

If the crowd hesitated, he might say, "Oh! Come on now! Not even a dollar? Will anybody give fifty cents for this beautiful lamp?"

Finally, a shy farm wife might wave her hand and nod.

"There you go! Now I got halfa dollar for the lamp, who'll make it a dollar, a dollar, a dollar, dollar, who'll gimme a dollar?"

"Yep!" a man yells from the back.

"Now we gotta dollar, now put it up to two. Gotta dolla, gotta dolla, gotta git in for more. Who'll make it two, two, two? Wanta git in, gotta make it two, put it up, put it up, put it up! Two dollars!"

Another bid comes in for two, and the chanting and bidding goes on. No more bids come after four-fifty and the bidding stops. "I got four-fifty, who'll make it five? Five, five, five, five? It's a beautiful lamp. You'll love it. Somebody give five dollars? Five dollars? Going, going, gone! Sold to the lady in the pink dress for four and one-half American dollars! A lucky lady!"

The chanting, bidding, and buying could go on all day, into the mid-afternoon. The festivities might be lubricated by coffee, doughnuts, and sandwiches sold by church ladies at a table to the side. Neighbors who seldom saw each other this close up would chat about the weather and the crops over hot coffee and fresh doughnuts.

Sometimes a widow sat on the porch beyond the crowd, weeping. Her husband might have died less than a year ago, and she was watching as her treasures of a lifetime were being handled and bargained for. People she barely knew were carting off things that had been so familiar they seemed like friends.

Finally, the auction was over. One household had ended, and the life of its last member was near an end. Other marriages and households were beginning with old objects that were new to them. And some of those auctioned items would become treasured friends until another auction, a greater one, fifty, sixty or more years later.

Howard Overmeyer was the Elmore auctioneer I remember, but I'm sure I saw and admired others. In my adult years, I wanted to become an auctioneer like Howard. I tried to learn an auction cadence, but by then I was too old.

(My grandmother, Emma Gleckler Kardatzke, held an auction a year or two after her husband Fred died in their home on Graytown Road. She, too, wept as she watched her household goods auctioned in the yard next to the Leatherport School building that had become Fred's garage and granary.)

31
Oil and Gas Wells

THE FARMS AROUND LEATHERPORT and Elmore were dotted with oil and gas wells. An oil well was on the south side of the big pond behind my family's house, and oil storage tanks sat on the grass a safe distance from the pond. At one time, the storage tanks held crude oil that trucks took to refineries in Toledo. By the time I was seven years old, oil production at that well had stopped, but gas from the well was still piped to Uncle George Gleckler's former house for cooking and heating.

An oil well sat next to the practice athletic field on the east side of the Elmore School. Oil was sometimes pumped from that well while we kids were in school. One day when I was in third or fourth grade, the oil well was pumping during recess. A ferocious-sounding gasoline engine was powering the pump from about two hundred yards away in a farm field. A long metal rod jerked back and forth through tall grass, driving the pump while the engine roared in the distance.

A kid on the playground saw the pump operating and the long metal rod leading to an engine shed. It was more exciting than a game of touch football. He yelled to another boy, and the word spread, and soon several of my class members went to investigate. The metal rod was jerking back and forth in tall grass, and the pump was doing its pump thing, but I especially recall that one of the girls said something memorable.

"There's a *queer* thing happening!" she said, gazing at the plunging steel rod. We all looked in wonderment.

I somehow knew the word she used, so I knew that she meant a strange thing was happening. But I had never heard anyone use that word in a sentence. I was impressed.

(George Gleckler's house was later occupied by the Viebrooks family and then by the Schwembergers. They used the gas from the pond-side well, too. Randy Ross bought the house in the 1990s. The gas probably ran out long before he moved in.)

32
Making Hay

ONE SUMMER DAY, I WAS PLAYING outside at my grandparents' farmhouse while Mama was inside talking with Gramma. It was a quiet, calm, sunny summer day. I looked up from my play just in time to see something beautiful coming down the lane on the other side of the apple orchard. It was huge, and it became larger and larger, like a cloud being blown silently or like a hot air balloon floating along at ground level.

As it came closer, I could see that it was a tall wagonload of loose hay pulled by a big brown horse. The horse's hooves clip-clopped along the dusty lane making little dust clouds with every step. Silver buckles gleamed on the horse's neck and shoulder harnesses. Delicate streamers of hay hung over the sides of the wagon, some dangling nearly to the ground. High on the pile of hay a man guided the horse with long leather reins.

The hay wagon looked majestic as it made the turn at the edge of the orchard, and it went right in front of where I was playing. The only sound in the warm summer air was the clip-clop of the horse's hooves. The wagon and hay slid by me almost as quietly as a cloud. When it arrived at the barn, men were there to lift the hay by ropes and pulleys high into the hay mow.

The hay was dry and dusty, but the cows in the milking shed and the steers in the feed lot didn't care. They would contentedly munch on the hay in the coming winter. I didn't think I would like to eat it, even if I were a cow or a steer. As a boy, I didn't have the teeth or the special four-part stomach of a cow. Grampa had told me he had to be sure the hay was dry before it went into the barn or it would rot. Rotting hay could mold and get hot, and if it became hot enough, it could catch fire and burn the barn down. Maybe that's why farmers believe the saying, "Make hay while the sun shines."

33
Apple Butter Time

It was in about 1944 when I first saw apple butter being made on a cold fall day in Uncle Harris and Aunt Delorous' yard on the River Road. Women from my church looked like old-time German farm wives toiling over a cooking pot in their long, heavy coats. Scarves covered their heads, and some warmed their hands in their pockets.

When my mother and I arrived, a big fire was burning under a black pot so large that three or four kids could have played in it if it hadn't been full of apple butter. Logs were there to keep the fire going all day. A small cloud of steam swirled up from the pot, and when the wind blew just right, you could smell apple cider and cinnamon and apples seething there together.

I watched a woman wielding a long pole with the board on its end like a large wooden hoe on a very long wooden pole. The board reached down inside the pot to stir the apples and cider as they cooked. She took turns with other women pushing the pole, stirring the apple butter. The scene seemed like something from the Old Country, even from medieval times and the women looked like German ancestors of Leatherport folk.

Most of the women there that day actually *were* German farm wives, since many Leatherport families were of German ancestry. Some may have seen their parents or grandparents make apple butter this way back in the Old Country.

The apple butter pot simmered all day, but I was a little kid and couldn't stay to see the actual apple butter when it was scooped out of that big black pot. I was just glad I had seen and smelled apple butter cooking over a rosy, smoky fire on a cold fall day. I never had another chance.

34
A Trip to the Cider Mill

THE CIDER THAT WENT INTO home-brewed apple butter came from nearby orchards on Graytown Road. Making apple cider was an industrial process of its own and well worth remembering.

When I was in high school, I tended the family orchard as part of my training to be a farmer. "What is so rare as a day in June?" asked the poet. But I might have asked, "What is so rare as a day in October?" October was truly a time of rare, beautiful days.

One of those beautiful October days came after the good apples had been picked and stored for winter. Only wormy, bruised, and half-rotted apples were strewn around the orchard, and they were perfect for cider. My dad had a day off from his work at the refinery, and he said it was a good day for a trip to the cider mill.

We decided to use the ancient Avery tractor I had bought a year earlier from a farmer nearby. We loaded two large wooden barrels and lots of one-gallon jugs into the trailer. We drove between the piles of apples, scooping them up with our grain shovels and dumping them into the barrels. When we finished loading, my dad climbed into the trailer with the apples, and I drove the tractor and trailer out onto Graytown Road heading north.

The morning was still cool, typical of October mornings, but bright sunshine warmed us as we puttered along as fast as the little tractor would go. It took nearly forty-five minutes to reach the cider mill at our speed, but we felt it was almost like a hayride in broad daylight.

The cider mill looked like a barn, but the sweet smell of crushed apples was nicer than the usual barn smells. I drove up to an open window, and a cheery lady greeted us there.

"Just dump them apples in the chute," she yelled over the sound of an apple-grinding machine. You'll get your cider over there." She motioned toward a loading chute and a pipe coming from the side of the building. We dumped our bruised, wormy apples into the loading chute and pulled ahead to the discharge pipe.

In a few minutes, amber-colored cider was flowing into the jugs. When the jugs were filled, the rest of the cider went into the barrel. My dad pulled some bills from his pocket for the woman in the window, and off we went.

We drank some of the cider that day and sold some of it. We drank cider in the evenings with our popcorn most evenings in the next week or two, celebrating the delicious cider we had made from rotten, wormy apples. We never thought once of the crushed worm juice we must have swallowed.

35
"Who Closed the Stanchions?"

———❖———

I COULD HAVE BEEN IN BIG TROUBLE at Gramma and Grampa's house one evening if they hadn't loved me so much and forgiven me. I did a bad thing.

At milking time after supper, Gramma and Grampa and I walked from their white farmhouse out to the big red barn. Inside the barn, we walked past the big piles of hay and the stalls where the horses slept. The barn's dusty smell made this an adventure in the world of grown-up work, and I loved it. I felt lucky to be with them because I had never been inside the barn at milking time.

When we reached the milk shed at the back of the barn, Gramma walked down the long row of tall metal clamps in front of the feed trough. Gramma clicked open the clamps one by one, but I didn't know why. I just liked the clicking sound. Grampa filled the feed trough with buckets of oats and ground corn. Then they both went out into the barnyard and I stayed inside.

While Gramma and Grampa were outside, I decided to see how the metal clamps worked. I walked down the feed trough and, one by one, clicked them shut. Click, click, click, click. It was a lovely sound. Click, click, click. All six clamps were locked shut.

Suddenly, before I understood what was about to happen, a cow came into the milk shed. Then there was another. All the cows were coming in. The first cow went to the far end. She turned in toward the feed trough. Bonk! She bumped her head on the locked clamp in front of her. I heard the same sounds as each of the cows did the same thing: bonk, bonk, bonk, bonk, bonk.

The first two cows decided they must have made a mistake by trying to come in to be milked. They backed out of their stalls and tried to squeeze past the other puzzled cows that were still coming in. None of the cows trying to come in knew why the others were going out, but they tried to turn around and go back out, too. Cows were coming and going and bumping into each other.

The next thing I saw was Grampa and Gramma running into the milk shed.

"Who closed them stanchions?" Grampa asked, looking directly at me.

I wondered what he meant. I didn't know the word "stanchions."

Gramma pushed past the cows to get to the feed trough, and she began to unlock the clamps I had just shut. "Clonk, clonk, clonk," the stanchions seemed to say as they were popped open.

Oh, no! I thought. *Those things are the stanchions! That's what I made click!*

"Who closed them stanchions?" Grampa asked again, looking at Gramma and me.

Gramma didn't say anything. She was sure she hadn't done it. My heart was pounding.

"Who closed them stanchions?" Grampa asked a third time. He didn't sound happy.

I was trembling. I was too scared to say anything else, so I said, "I don't know."

Neither Grampa nor Gramma said anything more. They just finished opening the stanchions, and the cows obediently took their places. Gramma clicked the stanchions shut again, this time with a cow's neck in each one. As I watched, I could see that the stanchions fit next to the cows' necks but didn't pinch them or hurt them. The cows' heads were wider than their necks, so they couldn't pull out when the stanchions were closed.

Grampa got out his bucket and his three-legged stool and sat down next to the first cow. I watched as he began milking.

"We better go back to the house," Gramma said.

I looked at Grampa milking. Gramma had the right idea. Grampa wasn't smiling. He pressed his head against the side of the cow and looked down at the foaming milk in the bucket and milked extra hard. He didn't look at me.

Gramma and Grampa never scolded me or got mad at me for locking the stanchions, and I don't think they ever told Mama and Daddy. They probably laughed about it that night after I went home. They might have felt angry at first, but they never let me know it. They just acted as though they really didn't know who closed the stanchions. I'm still thankful they forgave me that night.

(Students in school or college usually sit in the same seats every day, even if their places aren't shown on a seating chart. Grown-ups in church almost always sit in the same place Sunday after Sunday. These people remind me of the cows taking their regular places every day in the milking shed. For some reason, people like to sit in their regular places, but thankfully they don't need stanchions to hold them in place once they get there.)

36
The Milk Cat

GRAMPA HAD A TALENTED CAT that went with him to the milk shed every morning and night when he milked the cows. If the cat had a name, I never heard it. But I saw the cat every time I saw Grampa milking his cows. Grampa didn't have many pets, but he liked this cat. It was more like a farmhand than a pet to him.

I loved being at Grampa's house at milking time. It was amazing to see the huge cows walk into the milk shed and stick their heads into the stanchions, a word I learned in another story. I was only about three feet tall, but the cows were over five feet tall, and they seemed to be ten feet long. Each time the cows entered the milk shed, they went to the same places. I wondered if they were smart enough to line up outside so each cow could easily get to her place. I never checked.

Even though the cows were huge, they seemed to like Grampa and obeyed him and let him milk them. He milked them every day, in the morning and in the evening. I never saw Grampa milk in the morning because I was just having breakfast at my house then. But I saw him milk the cows enough times at night to know it was a good show.

The milking shed was just big enough for Grampa's six cows. There was a feed trough in front of each cow, and there was a "bathroom trench" behind each cow. While the cows were in the stanchions, sometimes they had to "go" while they were still in the milking shed, and they could use the bathroom trench. I learned the hard way to be careful not to get too close when I walked behind the cows.

The cows ate contentedly while they were being milked. I thought their snack at milking time probably made the milk taste better. Grampa pressed his head against a cow as he milked her. She probably was comforted by feeling his head there and by the swish, swish, swish, swish sound of her milk splashing into the big metal milk bucket.

Grampa's milk cat kept him company almost every time he milked the cows. It would hang out in the barn and watch for Grampa to come with his milk buckets. The milk cat must have liked to hear the swish, swish, swish of the milk, and it always watched from the other side of the cows' bathroom trench. The cat knew to stay away from the back of a cow. A cat could never be sure when a cow might kick or go to the bathroom.

When he was milking, Grampa would look to his left across the bathroom trench to the cat. "Want some milk, Kitty Cat?" he'd ask.

The cat would sit up and look at Grampa, waiting for some milk.

"Here comes!" he'd say.

Grampa would point a nipple at the cat and squirt a solid stream of warm milk, straight into the cat's open mouth. The cat gulped the milk as fast as it could, and only a spilled a little. I laughed and clapped my hands for the cat when she caught the milk in her mouth.

One time during milking Grampa turned to me. "How 'bout some fresh milk for you? It don't get no fresher than this," he said.

He pointed a nipple at me, and before I knew it there was warm milk all over my face and clothes. I licked a little off, and it tasted good. Grampa was laughing.

"Wanta try it agin? You missed some that time!" he said.

I shook my head and laughed and wiped the milk from my face.

"I guess we better leave that trick to the milk cat," he said, and gave the cat another squirt of milk. The cat slurped it down again right out of the air. "See that?" he asked. "Next time, maybe you can do that."

I looked at the cat, and the cat looked at me. The cat seemed proud of itself. It almost seemed to be saying, "I can catch milk in my mouth, and you can't. I can catch mice, and you can't. If I fall out of a tree I always land on my feet, and you don't."

I didn't mind if the cat was making fun of me. The cat was right, but I knew I could already do some things that a milk cat couldn't do.

37
Separating the Cream and Making Butter

MILK STRAIGHT FROM A COW is a blend of milk and cream. If raw milk sits without stirring for a few hours, the cream separates from the milk and floats on top of the milk. Farmers found they could sell cream and milk separately. Sometimes family farms sold only the cream and kept the milk. Cream could be churned into butter, and cream was more valuable than milk. There was less cream, so it was easier to truck the cream away to town to sell. Excess milk was sometimes carried to the barn and fed to the hogs.

At old-time farms, cream could be separated from milk by a machine called a cream separator. It was a tall machine that stood on the floor. At Gramma and Grampa's farm, Gramma did the work of separating the cream from the milk. I watched her pour milk into the cream separator and then turn the crank. When she cranked, the creamy milk began to spin slowly, then faster and faster. The machine whined at a high pitch. Milk flowed from one of the separator's stainless steel spouts into a milk bucket. Cream came out another spout into a smaller bucket.

The milk that went to the hogs was often mixed with grain or other food to create what was called "pig slop." "Slopping the hogs" was a happy chore on the farm, especially for the hogs. They clamored for slop and jostled each other aside for the best places at the trough making oinky and squealy piggish sounds. The pigs were even happier than the one who brought the slop.

City folk may think "pig slop" is something disgusting or even unsanitary. There's a degree of truth to that because table scraps, potato peels, and other kitchen food by-products were sometimes included in the slop. But the slop made only of ground grain mixed in milk or water looked like breakfast cereal and smelled so good that farm kids would have liked to taste it. Maybe some did.

Cream that was kept on the farm could be poured over corn flakes for breakfast or into coffee for grown-ups. Cream could also be made into butter by simply churning it in a butter churn. My grandma's butter churn was a big glass jar with a handle on the top attached to a gear and a wooden mixing paddle down in the cream. Turning the crank caused the paddle to spin inside the jar and stir the cream. Just stirring very thick cream turns it into butter. I know it works, but I don't know why.

In much earlier times, butter churns were tall wooden tanks. Butter was churned by a plunger inside the tank with an up-and-down motion. It must have been because of those churns that a short kid was sometimes described as "knee-high to a butter churn." But some people are quick to say, "Butter churns don't have knees."

(The milk in stores doesn't separate like fresh cow milk because it has been homogenized, but butter can still be made at home. You can churn your own butter by putting some heavy cream from the grocery store in a glass jar and shaking it. Before long there will be globs of unsalted but delicious butter in the jar. Be sure to close the lid on the jar before you shake it.)

38
The Riding Pig

ONE EVENING MY FAMILY DROVE to Grampa's house to get fresh milk from his cows. On the way, Daddy said, "Who would like to ride the riding pig tonight?"

"I want to! I want to!" Owen and I both yelled. It sounded like wonderful fun.

My brother Owen and I had seen the riding pig, the one Grampa treated as a pet even though it lived in the barnyard with the cows, chickens, and other pigs. Because he petted it and talked to it, the pig had become so tame, Grampa said, that a small boy could ride on its back.

We arrived at the evening milking time. The big barn was dark, but we could see a light at the back in the milking shed. Grampa was milking, just as we thought. Daddy led us through the barn and into the milking shed to ask Grampa about riding the pig.

We kids loved the smell of hay and animals in that barn. We liked to see the cats and chickens that were sometimes hiding inside and the birds that made nests up high. We knew there were bats hanging upside down up high, too, and they seemed so scary we hoped they wouldn't fly down on us.

"Well! You brought your helpers!" Grampa said, laughing as we walked into the milking shed. He was just finishing the milking, and he brought two foaming pails of still-warm milk to the door where we were standing. He set the pails down and looked us over, smiling like Santa with his rosy cheeks. It felt good that Grampa noticed us. It made us feel big and important.

"We'd like to get some fresh milk," Daddy said, "and the boys are wondering if they can ride the pet pig."

"Shore can," Grampa said. "I got plenty 'a milk, and I just seen that pig. Let me get these cows outa here first."

Grampa walked along where the cows' heads were clamped between the metal bars that made them stand still while they were being milked. One by one, he unlocked the stanchions that held their heads, and each huge, ponderous cow backed out of its stall and lumbered for the door into the muddy back barnyard.

When the last cow had left, Grampa went to the door and looked for the pet pig among the other pigs and the cows. It was on the other side of the barnyard, so he called to it. "Whooo, pig! Whoooeee, pig!"

The pet pig raised its head from where it was rooting. She was glad to see Grampa because he was her pal, and she jumped in the air, squealed with delight, and ran toward us. Pigs have a strange, bucking way of running when they try to run fast. We laughed to see a pig running to us like a pet dog, especially when it ran so funny.

"She's really ready to play," Grampa said as the pig ran to him and stood there while he patted her. "Now, who'll be the first to ride? How about the little guy first?"

Without another word, Grampa picked up Owen and lifted him above the pig. The pig stood still, sniffing the ground where the cows had just passed through. Grampa lowered Owen gently onto the pig's back. I watched carefully, knowing I would be next. I could see that the riding pig's back was rounded, so there was really no place to sit safely and no way to hang on.

In case you don't know much about pigs, their backs are not flat like those of horses and cows. Pigs' backs are rounded because pigs spend so much of their time with their noses on the ground, rooting and digging for things to snack on like roots, seeds, bugs, and food dropped by other animals. Also, their backs have powerful muscles that help them lift heavy things with their noses, sometimes including fences that are supposed to keep them in.

Owen and I were about to find out that any place we sat on the pig's back would make us feel like we were about to fall off, which we were. If we sat too far forward, we were likely to fall over the pig's head, right where it was going to walk. If we sat too far back, we would fall off that end. I won't describe that end of the pig in detail, but I can say that falling off that end would not be pleasant.

As Grampa was about to take his hands off Owen, he got scared. "Don't let go, Grampa! Don't let go!" he yelled.

Grampa held onto Owen and nudged the pig to make it take a few steps. All the time, Owen kept making what I thought were just "scaredy-cat" noises. I could tell he was about ready to cry. I was bigger, so I knew I wouldn't be scared when it was my turn.

I could see what Owen was doing wrong. He was too near the pig's head, and he was about to fall off the front. He didn't have his hands on the pig's back to keep from falling forward, and he didn't have his feet squeezed against the pig's sides to hang on. I would do everything differently, and I would make the pig give me a good ride, maybe all around the barnyard and back to Grampa.

I could hardly wait for Owen to get off the pig so I could ride. "Put me on now, Grampa!" I said as he lifted Owen off. "I want a bigger ride! I know how to ride the pig!"

"Oh you do, do you?" Grampa laughed. "How do you know?"

"I was watching," I said.

"Okay, here you go!" he said as he picked me up and started to put me right where Owen had been sitting.

"Not there, Grampa," I said. "Put me farther back. Put me right at the top."

"How's that?" Grampa asked when he had settled me at the very top of the pig's arched back.

"Okay, Grampa, okay," I said breathlessly. "Let me go now. I can ride by myself."

Grampa was chuckling as he let go of me and stepped back. The pig, with me aboard, just stood there, looking out into the barnyard.

I wanted the pig to go forward so I could have my big ride, so I squeezed my knees and feet against the pig's sides to hold on. I leaned forward a little so I could put my hands on the pig's back for balance. And then I gave the pig a little kick with my feet and rocked my body back and forth to make it move. In response to my nudging, the pig took a couple of steps forward into the muddy barnyard.

I was riding the pig! Everybody behind me was laughing and cheering!

After taking those few steps in the mud and manure, the pig stopped to look around. It was probably pleased with what it saw. It was a warm, friendly barnyard, filled with pig friends, slow-moving cow friends, and busy chicken friends. Suddenly the riding pig saw its favorite cow friend doing something across the barnyard. The other pigs saw it too. Pigs everywhere squealed and ran across the muddy barnyard.

Then something bad happened. It was so bad that I will remember it always. The riding pig let out a scream of excitement. "Arrreeeeeuuuuh!" it shrieked, and it burst forward.

Before I knew what was happening, I fell straight down, off the pig's back end. Splat! I landed in the mud and manure. I looked up just in time to see the riding pig win the race across the barnyard. What a fast pig!

Everybody laughed. They laughed so hard they could hardly breathe.

Everybody was still laughing except me as I got up from the muddy manure. I knocked as much of it off as I could, but some was stuck on the seat of my pants. I was mad because everybody was laughing, but I was proud that I had almost ridden the riding pig across the barnyard as I had dreamed I might.

"What happened?" Grampa asked finally, still laughing so hard he was choking for breath. "What happened, did the pig throw you off?" he asked again after another guffaw.

Daddy spoke next, still laughing too. "I guess that was a bucking pig, and she threw you off!"

His words really made me mad. The pig didn't throw me off. I was riding just fine until it ran out from under me. "Nope," I muttered. "The pig just ran away!"

I didn't look at Grampa or Daddy. I walked right past them and into the barn, burning with embarrassment. They laughed again, and we all walked through the barn and back to the milk house, where Grampa filled our one-gallon jars with milk.

We watched Grampa pour the rest of the fresh milk into the metal milk cans that were bobbing in cold water in the deep concrete sink in the milk house floor. The milk truck would come the next day and take those big cans to town. A train would then take the milk to a place to be sterilized and put into jugs to sell to people in big cities like Toledo and Fremont so kids could have milk on their corn flakes just like us.

When everyone was done laughing and talking about my ride on the pig, we walked out to the car. Daddy and Owen got in.

"You better stand up," Daddy said to me, "so you don't get dirt on the seat." I stood up in the back, holding on to the front seat, until we arrived at our house.

I'll never ride another pig, I said to myself. And I never did.

39
Hiding in a Corn Shock

———※———

CORN SHOCKS WERE COMMON around Leatherport when I was a small boy. Back then, some of the field corn was cut and gathered by hand to feed to cows and to use for their beds. The cornstalks needed to be dried so they wouldn't mold before the cows ate them or slept on them. The cut cornstalks were stacked in teepee-like towers and left in the fields to dry. When I was about five years old, I helped my dad and my Uncle Harris "shock some corn."

To make the teepees, the men started with stalks of corn still rooted in the ground. They pulled the tops of several stalks together and tied them with strong string. They cut other stalks and tilted them against the bundle of rooted ones. When there were enough stalks to make a good-sized tee-pee, they tied all the stalks together in a bundle at the top.

The teepees made nice little houses for small kids who happened to be out in the field. I mainly helped the men by staying out of their way, hiding in the corn shocks. I'd find a crack in the side of a shock and squeeze inside. On a cold, windy day, it was a snug place to hide while the full-grown men were making more corn shocks. Sometimes I shared my corn shock with a field mouse or two, but they were tiny and friendly and didn't take up much space.

Grandpa Fred with fellow hunters and a rabbit; the kids are Nyle, Merl, and Owen. The former Leatherport School is behind them.

40
The Joy of Chasing Chickens

I WASN'T ALWAYS WELL BEHAVED when I was a small boy (and I'm still not always good), but I remember a day when I was a "good boy" by accident. I was happy about what I did that day even though I wasn't trying to be good on purpose.

When I was about four years old, I was at Gramma and Grampa's house one day while my cousins Denny and Jack were there. They were living with Gramma and Grampa because their dad, my Uncle Jim, was away in the war. The day was bright and cool, probably in October. It was a good day to be on the farm with Gramma and Grampa and Denny and Jack.

That morning, Grampa decided to go for a walk around the farm buildings. He may have felt that he needed to check on something out there.

Maybe he just wanted to get out of the house for a little while. Maybe Gramma wanted him to take us boys out of the house so she could do her work. We three boys might have been running around in the house making a lot of noise, but we wouldn't have noticed. It was our own noise. It's only big people who notice when boys are noisy.

We three boys and Grampa put on our jackets and went out on the big, wide driveway past the garage toward the corncrib. Jack was the littlest, and Grampa picked him up as we walked. Denny and I were glad to be walking so we could walk or run or maybe even skip or jump over sticks that needed jumping over.

After a few minutes, we came to the big, wide wooden gate that could swing open to let the tractor and plow go out to the fields. Grampa untwisted the wire that held the gate shut and swung it open for us. After everyone had gone through, he made sure the gate was closed. There were pigs and cows behind the gate, and they might have wanted to escape.

None of us saw pigs or cows that day, but we did see chickens—what I thought of as big, white, stupid, scaredy-cat chickens that usually needed to be chased. They were pecking the ground because that's what chickens do: They peck at things like seeds and bugs and worms.

Most animals were bigger than me when I was four, and I was scared of them. Not the chickens. I was bigger than them, and I could scare them. The best thing was to run at them, waving my arms like I was going to fly, yelling, "Wooo! Wooo! Wooo! Chickens! Run, chickens! Run!"

Even though I thought all chickens were stupid, they must understand English. When I yelled, "Run, chickens run" and ran at them, they ran. They even flew a little way. It was fun to run into a flock of clucking chickens and make them squawk and scatter in all directions. Afterward, a cloud of white feathers settled on the grass where the chickens had been.

Grampa's chickens had only two ways to get even with me for chasing them. One way was to poop on the lawn so I would step on it. I was barefoot most of the summer, so the poop would squeeze between my toes, and *that* was *nasty*, even for a boy. The other way they got even was to peck my hands or arms when I tried to pull eggs out from under them in the chicken coop.

A good day for chasing chickens would be a day when Grampa was out in the fields and Gramma was busy in the house. But this day, Grampa was with us, and he didn't like his chickens to be chased. He saw Denny and me looking at the chickens pecking the ground in front of us. He knew what we were thinking, so he looked down at us and said in a firm voice, "Don't chase the chickens!"

We knew we weren't supposed to chase the chickens, but it was a good thing he reminded us. We just watched those stupid, scaredy-cat chickens hopping and skipping along in front of us in their chicken way, not getting the good scare they deserved. We really wanted to chase the chickens, but Grampa had said, "Don't chase the chickens!"

Just to be sure we heard him, Grampa said again, a little louder, "Don't chase the chickens!"

Denny and I followed Grampa and Jack behind the corncrib and out toward the machine sheds and the big barn. I took another look at the chickens and noticed how much they needed to be chased. But then I saw a whole bunch of pigeons landing on top of the corncrib. I looked up and watched the pigeons circle around and land. They waddled along the peak of the corncrib roof and talked to themselves in their silly, warbling pigeon talk. The sky was blue, and I wondered where I would fly if I were a pigeon. I wondered if I would fall off the roof of the corncrib if I landed there. I wondered if I would still talk like a boy if I was a pigeon, or maybe I would talk that silly pigeon language.

I looked back down at the chickens. We were close to them, but I was still thinking about the pigeons, not the chickens. Denny was thinking only about the chickens. He got so excited he couldn't stop himself. He started running at the chickens, waving his arms in the air.

"Wooo! Wooo!" Denny yelled at the chickens.

I stopped thinking about the pigeons and took half a step to run after Denny and the chickens, but then I heard a very, very big voice say, "Don't chase them chickens!"

I looked up and it was Grampa. He didn't look happy. His face looked red, and he was staring at Denny.

Denny stopped running and stood still, like Grampa must have stopped him with his voice. I looked at Denny and was glad I wasn't him. Denny had been bad, chasing the chickens right after Grampa had told us both not to. If I hadn't been looking at the pigeons, I would have chased the chickens, too. I had been good by accident, thanks to the pigeons.

Grampa looked at me, and he probably knew that I had nearly chased the chickens too. He was still looking at me when he said, "He don't mind good, does he?"

I looked at Denny still standing still, and I was glad I wasn't him. I said to Grampa in a very grown-up way, "Nope."

I felt grown-up. I was older than Denny, and I hadn't chased the chickens, and I had a chance to show Grampa I was against chasing chickens the way Denny had.

Denny came back to us, and we all went on around the barn to the pasture. The cows were there. They didn't scare us, but we had to be careful not to step in any of their cow pies.

When we got back to the house, Gramma was baking cookies, and the house smelled wonderful. I looked at Denny, and Denny looked at Grampa. We both hoped that Grampa wouldn't say anything to Gramma about Denny chasing the chickens.

"Can we have some cookies?" is all Grampa said. He didn't say a word about the chickens, and neither did we. The cookies tasted especially good that day.

41
Free-Range Chickens

AT GRAMPA'S HOUSE, CHICKENS RANGED freely across the lawns, into the orchard, around the barn and outbuildings, and out to the edges of the farm fields. They constantly pecked at the ground, eating seeds and bugs to produce eggs and chicken meat. They sometimes found hard kernels of yellow field corn near the corncrib. They ate tiny stones in the gravel driveway and on the gravel road in front of the house. They were what modern city people call "free-range" chickens, and they ranged even more freely at Grampa's house than their modern relatives.

Gramma sometimes let me go to the chicken coop to gather eggs. It was an easy job, and it was fun to find eggs in the cubbyholes where the hens laid their eggs. Sometimes I had to scare a hen off its nest to collect the eggs.

Once there was an especially big hen that I couldn't scare off. I tried sliding my hand under its fluffy feathers to find eggs, but she pecked me with her sharp beak. Pecks on the hands were enough to scare off most kids like me. Grampa said that angry, pecking chicken was a "sitting hen," and I could see why. A sitting hen wanted to sit on her eggs until they hatched into baby chickens. That was the way farmers could get more chickens for eggs or meat, and it still works today if sitting hens are allowed to sit on their eggs long enough.

On our way home from church one Sunday, we were passing Gramma and Grampa's house when Daddy said, "Oh, no! Look at the chickens in the road!"

We all looked ahead at the road in front of Grampa's barn, and there were two fluffy white chickens lying in the road, splattered with blood. Bright red blood spotted the white limestone road too.

"Looks like they haven't been there long," Mama said. "We better take them home and clean them for dinner."

Daddy picked up the chickens and held them out the window with one hand to keep the blood out of the car. He drove the rest of the way home with one hand. When we got home, Daddy cut the heads off the chickens and pulled off the feathers. Mama cut them up and got them ready to cook. Our dinner was late that day, almost 2:00 in the afternoon, but we felt it had been a happy accident, and we were glad to have fresh chicken.

That afternoon after dinner, Daddy went to Grampa's house and paid him $1 for the two chickens. After all, even though they had been running free on the road, they were not "free" chickens for us.

(Sometimes people say something is "rarer than hen's teeth" because hens don't have teeth. They can't chew food in their beaks because the food would fall out. Chickens have something inside called a gizzard. It's a muscle that food goes through, and the food is "chewed" there by the gizzard muscle. Chickens eat sand and tiny stones that serve like teeth in the gizzard to chew up kernels of hard field corn and whatever else chickens manage to pick up with their beaks. Some people like to eat gizzards, and you can buy them in grocery stores. After all, gizzards have no bones, fat, or feathers.)

42
Hog Butcher for the World

Hog Butcher for the World,
Tool Maker, Stacker of Wheat,
Player with Railroads and the Nation's Freight Handler;
Stormy, husky, brawling,
City of the Big Shoulders:
From "Chicago" by Carl Sandburg, 1914

NO ONE COULD ACCUSE Leatherport of being the leading hog butcher for the world. Hogs might have been shipped as far away as the state line, but most of the Leatherport hogs stayed in Leatherport. The hogs that were butchered in Leatherport usually were eaten there as well.

The two roads that met in downtown Leatherport never ran red with the blood of hogs, as they supposedly did in Chicago, but blood did flow on butchering days at the nearby farms. Butchering day was a big event on any farm, and it was a life-and-death drama played out on any hog farm in the country in those times.

In late October of 1944, the weather had been cooling for a few weeks. The leaves had changed color and most had fallen from the trees. The temperature wasn't cold like winter, just cold like a typical late fall day with cold nights, frost in the morning, and chilly, sunny days.

One day when I was with Daddy at Grampa's farm, I heard Grampa say to Daddy, "Think you have time to help butcher a hog?"

I didn't know what Grampa meant, but I could tell by the look on his face and the tone of his voice that it was serious business.

Daddy looked around at the barn and corncrib, thought for a minute, and said, "Yep. I think I could. When d'y wanta do it?"

"I gotta check with Harris and Joe," Grampa said. "Be good to have at least one of 'em to help."

About a week later, Daddy said to me, "Want to come with me to Grampa's? We're going to butcher a hog today."

"Sure!" I yelled.

I ran to get my plaid coat and my hunter's cap with flaps to cover my ears, and Daddy and I headed for Grampa's house. I always liked to go to Grampa's farm. I thought that butchering hogs might be as much fun as riding a pig.

Gramma was always happy to see me. "Hi, there!" she said to Daddy when we came into the house. "I see you have your helper with you!" She looked at me and asked, "Are you ready to help the men butcher the hog?"

I stared at her a minute because I still didn't know what "butcher the hog" meant, so I just said quietly, "Yes."

Daddy asked, "Is Pa out in the barn a'ready?"

"Yep," Gramma said. "Him and Harris. Delorous dropped him off so she could keep the car today. I guess they wanta get started."

Daddy and I headed out across the lawn, past the little milk house and the corncrib, to the shed behind the barn. Grampa was there with Uncle Harris. A tractor was parked at the side of the shed, and the shed door was open.

"We a'ready got the sow in there," Uncle Harris said.

I looked in. A pig was penned by itself between a wooden gate and the wall. The pig was big and scary. I had seen pigs before, but I hadn't been this close to such a big one.

"You want to take over now?" Grampa said to Daddy.

I watched as Grampa handed Daddy his single-shot rifle. I had seen that gun before when Grampa shot it at a rabbit. The rabbit got away, but the bullet from the rifle made a big puff of dust near where the rabbit had been.

Daddy took the rifle and stood at the low wall right in front of the great big pig. The pig opened its mouth, squealed, and jumped toward Daddy. I thought it might bite Daddy or even eat him up.

"Better go ahead," Grampa said. "This one can be mean."

Daddy leaned over the gate and put the end of the rifle right against the pig's head. The rifle went "crack." The pig's knees buckled, and it dropped to the ground on its folded legs. It just sat there on the ground with its legs under it, not moving. Uncle Harris came into the shed. He opened the gate and rolled the pig to one side. He poked a big knife into the pig's neck, and blood poured out on the straw.

Daddy and Grampa pulled a long chain into the shed. They looped the chain on one of the hog's back legs.

Grampa went outside and started the tractor and backed it up to the shed. Uncle Harris attached the chain to the pig, and Daddy hooked the chain to the tractor so Grampa could pull the pig outside. The men rolled the dead pig onto a low wooden sled that was used for heavy things like this. I walked behind as Grampa's tractor pulled the pig to the corncrib.

Just inside the corncrib, a barrel of water was sitting on a smoky fire. Steam swirled up from the barrel. The men tied the pig's back feet to a rope that went to a pulley up high in the corncrib. Daddy and Uncle Harris pulled on the rope and dragged the pig slowly until it was hanging upside down over the barrel of steaming hot water. They lowered the pig head-first into the barrel. Hot water sloshed out and steamed up from the fire.

When the pig had soaked in the hot water, the men pulled on the rope until the pig came up out of the barrel about halfway. All three men started scraping the pig with wide, sharp knives. They were scraping off the tough hairs that grow on pigs like whiskers on a man's face. When half the pig was shaved smooth, Daddy and Grampa pulled the pig higher and started shaving the pig's front, all the way down to its nose.

By then I was tired, and the biggest excitement was over. I had seen the pig killed and bled and shaved. That was enough. I walked up to the house to see Gramma, and someone took me home for lunch and a nap.

Later that afternoon, Mama took me back to Grampa's farm. No one was in the corncrib anymore. The men had finished their work out there. Mama and I went into the house to see Gramma and whoever else might be in the kitchen.

"Did they get that hog cut up already?" Mama asked.

"Yep," Gramma said. "Took it to the locker to wrap up and freeze. Just left me with the sausage to make and some lard to render. They'll be back pretty soon."

Gramma kept working while she talked, cutting up meat and putting it into a large pile. Then she and Mama worked together, pushing pieces of meat into a large, metal meat grinder that was clamped to the edge of the kitchen table. Gramma stuffed big pieces of meat in the top, and Mama turned the crank. After a few turns of the crank, meat came out of the bottom of the grinder in long, pink strings and landed in a big pan on the floor.

When all of the meat had gone through the grinder, Gramma and Mama picked up the heavy pan together and set it on the table. Gramma dumped a lot of salt and pepper and some good-smelling spices onto the meat. Then she stuck her hands right into the chopped meat and mixed it up with her hands, squeezing handfuls of meat and salt and spices.

"Ever seen sausage getting made?" Gramma asked me.

I didn't even answer. I just stared.

"I'll take a turn at that, Mother," Mama said when Gramma got tired. Then Mama stuck her hands in the meat and mixed it more just like Gramma had done.

"That's good enough, Ruth," Gramma said after a while. "Let's start making the sausage so our little butcher here can see where his sausage comes from." She looked over at me. I felt important, but I wondered what she meant by "little butcher."

Next Gramma put a big, tall machine on the kitchen table. A metal tank at the top was open, and it had a pipe coming out its side at the bottom. Gramma and Mama both picked up big handfuls of the spiced, ground-up meat and dumped it into the top of the tank. When the tank was full enough, they put a heavy lid onto the top of the tank and locked the lid shut with clamps. A crank handle stuck out from the lid, and there were gears on the crank to push the lid down onto the sausage inside the tank.

Gramma went to the sink and brought back a long, soft tube. It was a piece of the pig's insides that the men saved from the butchering. She pulled one end of the tube over the pipe at the bottom of the tank and tied a string around the pipe to hold it on.

"Okay, let's take turns cranking," Gramma said.

Mama started cranking, and Gramma held the sausage tube. Sausage meat came oozing out the pipe into the tube. The tube was long enough to make several sausages. Mama kept cranking until the entire tube was filled with sausage meat.

Gramma slid the filled tube off the pipe and laid it on the table. She tied both ends with string, and then she tied it with string every five inches to make sausage links that were just the right size for cooking.

Mama got another long intestine tube from the sink and tied it on to the pipe like Gramma had done. It was Gramma's turn to crank this time. The two of them kept working and taking turns cranking until all the meat they had mixed had been used up.

That day I learned how a pig was butchered and how the sausage I liked to eat for breakfast was made from the pig. A few days later, Mama cooked some sausage and pancakes for breakfast. It was one of the best tastes I had ever had.

What I saw that day was a grown-up thing. I had never seen anything like it. The rest of that big pig, I learned later, was made into bacon, hams, pork chops, bologna, and hot dogs. And a kind of lunch meat called "head cheese" could be made from small pieces of the pig's nose and muscles in the pig's head. Even the pig's liver and heart could be cooked and eaten. Some farmers liked to say they used all of the pig but its "oink."

Every year when the weather turns cool in the fall, I like to tell people it would be a good day to butcher a hog. Most city people look at me as if I'm crazy or as if I'd said something impolite. They were never at Gramma and Grampa's farm to see how their sausage is made.

(Sausage that tastes like the sausage Emma Kardatzke made at her kitchen table in 1944 is available to purchase at Tank's Meats in Elmore, Ohio. Emma also made homemade noodles stuffed with boiled pork roast, onion, and sauerkraut. She called it "kraut kraupfa." It's the kind of thing my German ancestors may have eaten in the Middle Ages.)

43
Tony's Red Bread Truck

THE BRIGHT RED BREAD TRUCK came on Tuesday and Friday mornings at about 11:00 a.m. Scrolling letters on the side of the truck read "Tony's Bakery."

The driver was a jovial World War II veteran, and he loved his job. He always smiled and joked with us kids. We called him "Tony" because that's what it said on his truck and on the packages of bread and sweet rolls and doughnuts he brought.

"Hi, Tony!" we kids yelled whenever he pulled into our driveway. For us, it was like a small circus coming to our house.

"Hi! Come on, jump in and see what I've got!" Tony yelled to us excited kids.

He got out and slid open the truck's side door and we stepped into a heavenly aroma. The smell of fresh bread would have been enough, but there was more. Cinnamon and vanilla were in the air, and the smell of pecans and walnuts from the iced coffee cakes almost made us dizzy.

Mama couldn't buy everything we wanted, but sometimes she gave in to our begging and bought a coffee cake or a tray of cinnamon rolls along with the bread she needed for our breakfast toast and peanut butter sandwiches.

Our favorite kind of Tony's bread was the big, round Italian loaf. It had a delicious, tender crust, and the inside was like a white cloud. Mama sliced the bread into extra-large slices, half an inch thick and ten inches long. The slices were delicious plain, but they were even better with butter, peanut butter, and jam.

Tony's cinnamon rolls were among our favorite treats even though Mama made her own. We loved her cinnamon rolls, of course, but these were softer and came from the truck. They made Mama's regular baking easier if she had enough money to buy from Tony.

When we had all sniffed the bread truck and Mama had bought what she could, it was time for Tony to leave. He sometimes said, "Okay, I'm going to pinch your noses" and reached for a pair of pliers on the dashboard.

"No, no!" we'd scream and jump off the truck and run to the middle of the yard laughing. He'd laugh too. It was just another thing that made the bright red bread truck and Tony so much fun.

When Tony started the truck and backed onto the gravel road, he always beeped the horn a couple of times before his truck roared off to the north. A cloud of white dust chased him, and we watched until he was out of sight. Then we went inside to have some fresh bread and maybe some cinnamon rolls.

("In 1926, Anthony Szymanowski (1889–1965) bought the Sunshine Bakery next to his home at 709 White Road, Fremont, Ohio. Thus began Tony's Bakery, a Fremont household name for a half century that over the years grew to more than 300 employees. The family sold the business to Nickles Bakery in 1974, nine years after Szymanowski's death. Tony's Bakery is still recalled in Fremont today with many fond memories." — From an article by Larry Michaels and Krista Michaels that appeared on May 8, 2020, in the Fremont News Messenger*)*

Part Seven

People and Places around Northern Leatherport

44
The Neighborhood

IF YOU LIVE IN A CITY OR IN TOWN, you may be surprised that people who live out in the country also have neighbors even though their houses are far apart. In some rural areas, people can't even see their neighbors' houses. With fewer people to keep track of, people living in the countryside sometimes know more about their neighbors than those who live close to each other in houses or apartments in cities.

When my family moved to the pond house on Graytown Road in 1943, the Leatherport neighborhood stretched from Leatherport on Route 105 to Route 163 two miles to the north. The people we knew best lived on a one-mile part of Graytown Road between Gramma and Grampa Kardatzke's house and Babe Harmon's house just north of the La Carpe Creek.

If you look and listen wherever you go, you will find that every city, town, and village in the world has its stories. In every house there are happy stories and sad stories, dramas and conflicts managed or mismanaged by people inside. A few stories of those now-mythical Leatherport people and their homes have survived in local memory.

A "flivver" headed south past the Fred Kardatzke farm toward downtown Leatherport.

45
George and Mary Gleckler's House

UNCLE GEORGE AND AUNT MARY GLECKLER lived in a house on the south side of the pond that is still there on Graytown Road, though their house is gone now. George built the house in 1895 from brick he made in his backyard factory. His first wife and his oldest son were killed in a car-train crash in 1913, and the funeral was held in that family home. A few years later, Uncle George married a widow named Mary Steiner from Kansas, and they lived together in the house until Uncle George died there in 1945.

Uncle George's yard was beautiful. He planted flowers, grapevines, fruit trees, and a big garden. He tended hedges around the yard that made the house seem like his own little castle in a kingdom protected from the world by a green wall.

Whenever I visited Uncle George and Aunt Mary, there was a cozy smell from the thousands of wonderful meals that had been cooked there. Aunt Mary cooked on a stove that burned gas piped in from the old oil and gas well beside the pond.

Aunt Mary always had treats of dried apples, pears, peaches, and apricots from their trees. She dried the fruit on bedsheets in the yard on sunny days or on cookie sheets in her oven on rainy days. It was like candy to us kids. Aunt Mary also made tea from sassafras bark and roots she gathered from bushes in the woods across the road, but the tea was for grown-ups, not kids like me.

After Uncle George died, Skeeter and Nelly Viebrooks bought the house and moved in with their son John. His mother called him "Johnny," and she also called him "Jack" or "Jacky" as a nickname.

Johnny Viebrooks was a year ahead of me in school, and he seemed to come from a different world than most of the kids in the neighborhood. Not only had his family moved there from Toledo, but Johnny was also an only child. Most of the other families in the area had several kids. Another thing different about Johnny was that his parents smoked. They smoked a lot, and no one in my family smoked at all. As if those things were not enough to make Johnny strange and interesting to me, his mom was younger than my mother and had a louder voice than Mama.

On Johnny's first day of school in Elmore, his mother took him there in their little two-door, pre-World War II coupe. That was unusual, since my dad took our car to work and we always rode the bus. After that first day, Johnny rode the bus, too, and we often sat together on the school bus.

The most notorious escapade for Johnny and me was smoking together in the hog houses next to his house. No hogs lived in the hog houses then, and they were just being stored there by the farmer who owned them. The hog houses were clean enough for boys like us, and they were a good place to hide for a smoke. Johnny's parents had cartons and cartons of cigarettes in their kitchen, so Johnny could get smokes for us easily. He would sneak in and grab a few cigarettes when his mother was upstairs. We would go to our favorite hog house and light up. After we smoked, I would go to the pump in the old Leatherport School yard and rinse my mouth with cold water.

One day, I went along with Johnny to his house when he went for cigarettes. I waited outside while he went in the back door to the kitchen. Suddenly Johnny's mother yelled, "Jack-eeee!" She was screaming, and I couldn't hear the rest of what she said, but it was a lot. Outside at the back door, I was scared. I wanted to get away in a hurry. I don't think I ran, but I'm sure I walked home as fast as I could without attracting attention.

My family didn't have a phone yet, so Mrs. Viebrooks couldn't just call up my mother. If my mother ever heard from Mrs. Viebrooks about my smoking, she never said anything about it to me. After that day, I stopped smoking with Johnny Viebrooks. The Viebrooks family moved out in a couple of years, and my smoking days were over for a while.

The Schwemberger family bought the house and moved there in about 1947. Mark and Deloris had four kids. Peter was the oldest kid, followed by Susan, Ruthann, and Ellen. We kids played together and shared our pond and the old Leatherport School yard with the Schwemberger kids and the Sandrock kids, who lived in the house on the other side of us. Deloris Schwemberger died after the kids were grown, and Mark grieved her deeply before he died a few years later.

A man named Randy Ross bought the house from the Schwembergers. Randy put a lot of time and money into cleaning and updating the house and clearing the yard of extra trees and bushes and things Mark Schwemberger had collected. Randy upgraded the pond behind his house for swimming. In the dead of winter in about 2005, a fire broke out in a wood-burning stove in a new room on the west end of Randy's house. A strong westerly wind blew the flames through his house like a blowtorch, destroying it completely. Only a large metal storage barn remains to mark the place where the historic Gleckler house once stood.

(The story about the car-train collision that killed George's first wife and their son is told in my earlier book, The Clock of the Covenant *[2015].)*

46
The Gleckler-Beck-Sandrock-Aldridge House

MY FAMILY'S HOUSE WAS ON THE north side of the pond, and George and Mary Gleckler's house was on the south side, but an even older Gleckler house was on the north side of my family's property. It was a two-story brick house that had been one of the first houses on Graytown Road.

When my family moved into the pond house in 1943, the Walter Beck family was living in the house to our north. Walter and Alma Beck's sons Melvin and Jerry seemed like adult men to me, but they probably were just big farm boys. I didn't know the Beck's daughter, Betty. The Beck family moved out in about 1946.

The next family in that house was the Sandrocks. Earl and Donna Sandrock's kids were Roseanne, Wayne, Jane, Diane, Marcia, and Barry.

We were in different grades at school, but we played together a lot in all seasons of the year.

The creaking, old two-story house had become too old to repair, so in 1952 Earl Sandrock sold it to my dad for $200 to demolish and salvage. My family spent that summer tearing down the house and carting stuff to a storage area behind our garage. My dad salvaged lumber, paneling, bricks, and slate roofing. He used those materials for his projects for the rest of his life. The bricks had been fired on the property in the 1800s, and some were inscribed with names of Gleckler family members. John Gleckler's name was most common. A decaying pile of the ancient bricks was still on our family's property the last time I checked.

The Sandrocks built a white one-story house and that house is still standing and in good repair. The old barn and corncrib and other outbuildings are also still there as reminders of the earlier dairy farm.

We kids in my family had years of fun around the ponds and yards with the Sandrock kids and the Schwemberger kids. There were fifteen kids in all, counting the six in our family. The neighborhood swirled with activity in all seasons. We played baseball and touch football in the schoolyard in summer months. We swam and fished and skated at the pond. In the fall, we raked leaves and had bonfires together, almost like one big family.

(When I was a young kid, maybe four years old, I wandered over to the old Gleckler place beyond our orchard. We were way out in the country, and the barn and buildings were only about 100 yards from our house, so it was okay for me to go there. Uncle George had been tarring the flat roof on a shed. I found him sitting in the shade of one of the big maple trees with his pant legs rolled up and his feet in a bucket of water. I stood and gazed at the amazing sight for a minute or two. Uncle George looked up at me and then down at the bucket. "There are blisters down in that water now," he said, shaking his head. I didn't stay to see if the blisters floated on the water.

The current residents at the former Gleckler–Beck–Sandrock house are the Aldridge family. Jim Aldridge owns the large pond, and he bought the icehouse from our family just a few years ago.)

Gleckler family in olden times.

Some of the massive Gleckler family on the porch of their home-fired brick home: "Many hands make light work."

47
Mart Boss' House

MARTIN BOSS AND HIS WIFE MYRTLE lived a quarter mile north of my family's house, past the Sandrock home. They had two older daughters, Katherine and Bernice, plus sons named Ed and Fred. Ed and Fred were older than my older brother, and I did farm work for them while I was in high school.

When Mart Boss was alive, the family lived in a wood frame house that looked very old. After Mart's death, his son Fred built the white house that is still there. Ed Boss built a white frame house on the River Road in the very heart of ancient Leatherport.

Ed Boss had a heart attack and died on his tractor in a field on Kempke Road. Fred ran to his aid from another tractor nearby, but it was too late. Fred passed sometime later, but a member of the Boss family still lives on the farm.

48
Mart Boss and the Kites

ONE COLD, BLUSTERY DAY IN THE early spring, my two brothers and I were trying to fly kites over the field across the road from our house. It was probably late March or early April, and a strong wind was coming from the west. The wind blew across the flat farm fields and across the large pond that was behind our house.

At the time, my big brother Merl was probably only eleven years old, Owen was seven, and I was eight. We weren't good at flying kites. We had flown kites with Daddy before, so we had some idea of how to do it, but this time we were on our own. Daddy was at work at Sun Oil, and Mama was busy in the house.

With the wind at our backs, we three boys walked across the road in front of our house with our store-bought kites. There was a large, open field where the kites wouldn't get caught in trees or bushes. Even in that big field, we were having trouble getting our kites into the air and keeping them from crashing.

The kites were the traditional kind, made with paper shaped like two triangles, with points at the top, bottom, and sides. The trick in flying this kind of kite was to put it together just the right way. A thin wooden piece ran from the top to the bottom. A shorter piece made a "t" across the back of the kite, and it had to be bent slightly. If the shorter crosspiece wasn't bowed enough, the kite would just flop in the wind instead of flying. If it was bowed too much, the wood could break or not provide enough lift to make the kite fly. To fly a kite, a kid would hold on to a very long string tied in a special way to the kite. The kite would pull the string out longer and longer as the kite flew.

On that day of kite-flying, we didn't know about kite tails. A kite tail is a long, narrow strip of cloth or sometimes several strips of cloth tied together and fastened to the lowest point on the kite. The tail dangles in the wind under the kite and pulls the kite bottom down so the top points up and the kite flies straight. It's an important part of a kite that we didn't know. We just thought the strong wind would make our kites fly, no matter what.

Each of us had a kite to fly, and we each worked trying to get our kites into the air. Merl got his kite in the air first. Owen and I stopped our work for a minute to see Merl's kite jump up toward the sky, dart back and forth, and crash to the ground. It wasn't a happy sight.

Owen and I went back to work, hoping to make our kites work better than Merl's. When they were ready, we each let out some string and tossed our kites into the air. My kite went up a few feet and then made a dive for farmland. Owen's kite crashed at his feet the moment he tossed it in the air. We picked up our kites and tried again, but they crashed again and again. In the meantime, Merl was busy trying to untangle his string, so his kite wasn't flying either.

We could barely hear each other in the strong wind. All we could hear most of the time was the wind whistling through the ear flaps of our caps. None of us heard the small truck pull off the road and stop right behind us. Suddenly a loud, high-pitched man's voice yelled at us.

"You boys havin' trouble with them kites?" the voice nearly screeched.

We jumped and spun around. The voice was so loud and high-pitched and unexpected that we had jumped in fright. At first I didn't remember who the man was, with tanned cheeks, all bundled up in a ragged cloth farmer's coat. He wasn't a tall man, but he was big to us boys. He was smiling. Otherwise, he would have looked scary. It was Mart Boss, our neighbor from the second farm north of our house.

"You boys need some help?" he yelled in that same high-pitched, raspy voice.

We were still so surprised that we didn't know what to say, but Mart Boss didn't need us to say anything. He knew we needed help. He came over to me and picked up my kite.

"Let's see what we got here, Little Or," he yelled. He always called me "Little Or."

I was still scared of his voice, but I knew that Mart Boss was a nice man. I knew my parents liked him. He went right to work on my kite, adjusting the bowed piece in the middle. Then he looked at how I had attached the long string to the kite.

"We gotta fix this!" he yelled when he saw that I had simply tied my long string to the the middle of the kite. He broke the string and then made a length of string to attach at the top and the bottom the kite. Then he attached the long string and gave it back to me.

"Try that, Little Or," he said, turning to help Owen.

Merl was having more luck flying his kite, but it was still unstable. It darted back and forth and was always trying to crash. While Mart Boss was working with Owen, I launched my kite. It flew up pretty high, but it started dashing back and forth in the air like Merl's kite.

Mart Boss looked up at the two kites. "Hey! We gotta put tails on them kites!" he yelled.

To tell you the truth, Owen and I didn't know what a tail would be on a kite. We knew that our kitties had tails and birds had tails and Grampa's cows and horses had tails. We wondered how a kite could have a tail like the ones we knew about, so we just watched to see what Mart Boss would do next.

Mart just pulled a great big, red handkerchief from his pocket and started tearing it into narrow pieces in long strips. We had never seen a grown man do anything like that, tearing up his handkerchief. Then he tied the pieces of his torn handkerchief together in knots to make a long ribbon of red, knotted cloth.

"Howdya like that for a kite tail?" he said to me in his loud, yelling voice.

I didn't want to seem like I didn't know about kite tails, so I said, "Good."

"We'll see how good it works," he said, tying the tail to the bottom of Merl's kite. "Try it that way!"

Merl tossed his kite up into the gusting wind. It flew right up, higher and higher, catching the wind and standing tall and straight up in the sky, far out over the field. Merl let out more string, and the kite went higher until it looked tiny up there near the gray, fast-moving clouds.

Owen and I jumped up and down and cheered, and Mart Boss laughed in a high-pitched, happy laugh. He went back to his truck and came back with two rags that looked like they had once been women's dresses. He made two more kite tails, and soon all three kites were flying high above the flat farmland. We were busy watching our kites when we heard Mart Boss laugh and yell to us as he jumped into his pickup truck.

"Have fun, boys! Fly them kites!" he yelled.

Mart steered the little truck onto Graytown Road. We looked over our shoulders as he drove away, and he seemed to us like Santa Claus flying away after delivering gifts. We wouldn't have been surprised if we had heard him yell, "Happy flying to all, and to all a good kite!"

(*Mart Boss called me "Little Or" because my dad was nicknamed "Or." I was a grown man when I learned why my dad had that nickname. My dad's name was "Arlin," but when he was born, the doctor who filled out his birth certificate wrote his name as "Orlin" instead of "Arlin." Somehow everyone throughout Leatherport learned about this mistake. Some people began to call him "Or," and it became my dad's nickname, maybe because his hair was red like iron ore.*

My Aunt Elsie always called my dad "Or." Mart Boss knew my dad, so he gave me the affectionate nickname "Little Or," and I liked it. To me it meant I

Leatherport, Ohio

was a special friend of Mart Boss, like my dad was. Mart died on January 2, 1954, probably only six years after he helped us boys with the kites. He was only fifty-seven years old. He is buried in the cemetery at Elliston, Ohio.)

49
Mart Boss and the Pumpkins

I LEARNED TO RIDE A BIKE WHEN I was six years old in second grade. It was a "girl's bike," the kind where the middle bar goes down low so girls in dresses can ride. The low bar made it easy for boys like me to learn to ride a bike. I would start the bike rolling, hop up on the seat, put both feet on both pedals at the same time, coast a little, and start pedaling. Learning to ride a bike opened a world of adventure and danger to my brothers and me and later our sisters, who could ride bikes in dresses, but they usually rode in shorts or slacks.

I liked to ride my bike south on Graytown Road, past Grampa's house, and on toward the river. On other days I would ride the other way, north between farm fields past Sandrock's house and Boss' house to the La Carpe

Creek but not quite to Babe Harmon's house or the pea vinery. The road in either direction was perfectly flat because it had been laid on the floor of the former Black Swamp. It was an excellent place for kids to ride bikes.

Sometimes there were interesting things to see in the farm fields. You might see a combine cutting wheat and creating a cloud of dust. A tractor might be pulling a baling machine, and men on a wagon behind the baler would be piling golden bales of straw or green bales of hay on the wagon. Combines gathered up soybeans, and corn-picking machines munched their way through cornfields. Best of all, whole fields of pumpkins ripened in the fall, sprawled out like thousands of orange ornaments. I especially loved seeing the pumpkins because of their color and shapes and because they could be made into jack-o'-lanterns for Halloween, one of my favorite holidays.

One fall afternoon when I was still a beginner on the bike, I rode north to see what I could see. I turned onto Kempke Road, which we knew as the Half-section Road. I rode a quarter of a mile west and saw men working in a field of pumpkins. It was Mart Boss and his sons Ed and Fred.

"Hey, Little Or!" Mart Boss yelled as I bumped my way across the field toward the men.

They were busy cutting small pumpkins from vines and loading them onto a big farm wagon. These small pumpkins were the kind for pumpkin pie, and they would be sold to a cannery for pumpkin pie filling. I thought they would make good pumpkin faces, even though they were small. I watched the men awhile, and Mart Boss must have figured out what I was thinking.

"Wouldja like to have a punkin, Little Or?" he yelled to me.

I didn't want to seem selfish by taking a pumpkin, but I didn't want to miss out on a pumpkin either. I stood there without answering, looking at the pumpkins and wishing I could have one.

"How 'bout it? Ya want one?" he said again.

I nodded my head, but I was afraid to say anything around such big, strong farmers. Mart Boss stomped around the field in big steps until he found a pumpkin for me.

"How about this one?" he asked when he found one a little bigger than the others.

"Okay," I said, looking at the rather small pumpkin.

"Can ya put it in your bike basket?" he said. "Hey, you ain't got a basket, Little Or!"

I thought that would be the end of the pumpkin, so I picked up the bike and started pushing it through the bumpy field toward the road.

"Hang on, there, Little Or," Mart Boss called, stomping over to me with the pumpkin under his arm. "I got a way for you ta take the punkin home!"

He reached into one of the deep pockets of his bib overalls and pulled out a big pocketknife. He unfolded the big knife blade and cut a circle around the pumpkin's stem. Off came the top of the pumpkin, leaving a big hole. He marched over to where I was standing with the bike and slid the pumpkin over the end of one of the handlebars. The pumpkin started to slide off, but Mart Boss grabbed my hand and put it over the bottom of the pumpkin so I could hold it on, pressing the pumpkin onto the handlebar.

"There ya go, Little Or! Hold on to 'er!" he said. "Can ya ride home with yer punkin that way?"

I wasn't at all sure it would work, but I said, "Uh huh."

Mart Boss watched as I started walking the bike back toward the road. It was working, so I decided to ride the rest of the way over the bumpy clumps of grass. I was battling to keep the bike going fast enough when I hit the big bump at the edge of the road. Whoomp! The front wheel bumped up and slammed down, and the pumpkin split in two and fell with a splat onto the road. I put my hand on the slimy handlebar where the pumpkin had been and started to cry. I didn't want the men to see me crying, so I rode away as fast as I could.

By the time I got home, I had stopped crying. I wiped my face with my clean hand before going in the house, but Mama could see that I had been crying.

"What's the matter?" she asked.

I started to cry again. "Mart Boss gave me a pumpkin, but it broke."

Between sobs, I tried to explain the way I was trying to ride home with the pumpkin on the end of the handlebar and how the pumpkin broke when I went over a bump.

"That's too bad," she said. "Maybe we can get you another pumpkin later this fall. It was nice of Mart to give you one."

I didn't feel much better. All I could think of was my new, free pumpkin, splattered on the road. I went to another room and started doing my homework. I didn't hear someone pull into our driveway, but then I heard my mother talking to someone. I went outside to see who it was. It was Mart Boss.

"Looks like the boy had bad luck with his punkin!" he said in his special yelling voice. He then reached into the back of his truck and pulled out *two* pumpkins. Both were better than the one that had split in half and crashed to the ground.

I stared at Mart Boss and the two pumpkins.

"Here, take 'em, Little Or. Don't let 'em drop," he said, stepping over to me so I could take the pumpkins from his arms. They were so big that I had to take them from him one at a time. I set them down gently on the porch step and looked back up at Mart Boss.

"Don't you think you should say thank you?" Mama said.

"Thank you," I said, staring at the buttons on the front of Mart Boss' overalls. He let out one of his loud, high-pitched laughs but didn't say anything else.

"That was awfully nice of you, Mart," Mama said. "He will really enjoy those pumpkins."

"Yep. It's good he's got 'em," Mart said as he turned to get in his truck. "Maybe he can make one of them punkin faces with them. Maybe he can cook you a pie!" he said and laughed again.

Mart jumped back into his truck and drove away. By that time, it was already dark, but I knew he still had to milk cows and feed his pigs before supper. Every time I think of Mart Boss, I think of his wonderful kindness. He stopped his heavy farm work to help little boys and to replace my broken pumpkin. Somehow his rough farm style and his loud, high-pitched voice made his kindness all the more wonderful. I can never tell the stories about Mart Boss without tears in my eyes.

(*The Half-section Road was named for the fact that it was a half-mile north of the section line that ran along the south edge of the property where my family lived. A section is one square mile.*)

50
The Harmon House

"BABE" HARMON AND HIS WIFE Hilda lived a mile north of my family's house, just across the La Carpe Creek. Babe's real name was Clarence, but he always went by his nickname. Babe and Hilda were farmers and had a variety of chicken coops and barns around their place. They were so far from our house that we barely knew them, but we knew who they were.

The Harmons had one child, a daughter Eileen, who married and became Eileen Walterbach. She still lives in the Harmon house on Graytown Road, the same house where her family lived for so many years.

In 1977 I saw Babe and Hilda Harmon at an auction on Augusta Street in Elmore. I knew who they were, but I had been out of the area for nearly twenty years, so they wouldn't have recognized me. On June 30, 1977, I learned that Babe and Mrs. Harmon had been killed in a car crash on Route 163, not far from their Graytown Road home.

51
The Pea Vinery

---※---

THE PEA VINERY WAS A LONG, narrow machine that stood in a shed about twelve feet high. It was on the east side of Graytown Road, a short distance north of the Harmon house. In the vinery, field-grown peas were separated from the vines before the pea pods were sent to a packing house to be canned or frozen. I never saw the vinery in operation, but it must have been powered by a farm tractor with a belt attachment. It probably operated only in June and July each year when the peas, an early crop, were ready for harvest.

The pea vinery was a triumph of bad odor. As the pea pods were stripped from the vines, the vines themselves piled up into a heap next to the machinery. The vines stayed there for days, probably weeks, spoiling in the summer heat. That decaying pile of pea vines was one of the worst-smelling things I have ever known. If the wind was from the east, you could imagine purple and yellow-green odors writhing and drifting

Leatherport, Ohio

across the road like poison gas. Just to ride past the pea vinery in a car could turn your stomach.

You may cringe when you think of a muddy barnyard enriched with cow manure or a chicken coop where the chickens have made their deposits, but those are lovely smells compared to pea vinery "perfume." If the pea vinery were still there, and if there were a contest for nauseating smells, the pea vinery would take the prize.

52
Runaway One-Horse Open Sleigh

"Oh, what fun it is to ride in a one-horse open sleigh!"

MOST PEOPLE HAVE HEARD THE Christmas story about Santa and his sleigh, but not many have ridden in a sleigh. My Uncle Harris had a sleigh pulled by one horse, not "eight tiny reindeer." When I was only about five years old, I drove that sleigh.

Snow in Northern Ohio often comes off Lake Erie and roars across the flat farmland, creating huge snowdrifts. Sometimes the snow comes gently and covers everything with a soft white blanket. If snow comes gently during the night, the sun makes the roads and fields sparkle as though covered with millions of diamonds.

One snowy, sunny Saturday morning, my family was finishing a fine breakfast of pancakes and sausage and hot cocoa. There was a loud knock on the front door. It was Uncle Harris, bundled up in warm winter clothes, with his back to the blinding light of the morning sun. He was grinning.

"How did you get here, Harris?" my mother asked. "We didn't hear you drive up."

"'Course you didn't hear me," he said. "I come on my sleigh!"

Uncle Harris pointed over his shoulder to our front yard. We kids ran to the front window and could just barely see a horse and a large sled with two rows of padded seats. We knew it was a sleigh from pictures we had seen of Santa Claus and his sleigh.

"How 'bout I take them boys for a ride?" Uncle Harris asked.

My mother looked at us. "Want to go for a sleigh ride?" she asked. "You'll have to dress up warm. It's cold out there."

My brothers and I looked at each other, not knowing what to say, because none of us had ever gone on a sleigh ride. We hadn't even seen a sleigh until just a few minutes ago.

Mama looked at my brothers and me. "Want to go for a ride?"

"Yes," one of us said quietly, not quite sure what this would mean.

"Come on," Mama said, heading for our coats on the back porch. "Let's get you dressed to go out."

Mama helped us get bundled up in our coats, caps, gloves, scarves, and padded snow pants. When she had checked us over, we went outside where Uncle Harris was waiting beside the big, red sleigh.

"Who wants to go first?" Uncle Harris asked.

We three boys were silent, so he helped my big brother Merl get up on the front seat. He lifted my little brother Owen and me and placed us both on the back seat. Then he climbed up into the front seat and picked up long leather reins to drive the horse.

"Ready to go?" he asked.

Each of us looked at the edges of the sleigh and found places to hang on tightly. "Okay!" we all said at once.

"Giddyup!" Uncle Harris said to the horse, shaking the reins.

The horse leaned forward and began to walk, and the sleigh slid quietly across our snow-covered lawn, up the gentle slope to the road, and onto the snow-covered road. The sleigh's rails whispered softly over the snow. We could look straight north to where the road seemed to disappear against the sky.

Once again Uncle Harris said, "Giddyup," and this time the horse began to trot a little faster. Cold air whipped against our faces. About a half mile up the road, we turned around in the big, wagon-turning space in front of Mart Boss' barn. We headed for home, and our faces got colder and colder.

Back at our house, Uncle Harris turned the horse and sleigh around and stopped right in front of our porch again, pointing north as before. Uncle Harris said, "Whoa!" to the horse, and he helped us boys down.

"You folks want to go for a ride?" he asked my parents.

Daddy shook his head, and Mama said, "I'd better pass on that today, Harris. I'm not dressed for it."

While Uncle Harris and Mama and Daddy talked, we kids walked up and down the side of the horse and sleigh, looking it over. Then my big brother Merl went into the house and my little brother Owen went out to the back yard. I kept looking at the sleigh.

I could see the step that Uncle Harris had used to get up into the sleigh. I spotted a handle on the side to hold on to while getting up. The front seat looked high and fun to sit in. I pictured myself climbing up and sitting in the driver's seat of the sleigh.

No one was watching me, so I climbed up into the sleigh, just as I had pictured doing. It was just as I expected—a high seat behind a strong horse. I felt very grown-up and important. I thought about how Uncle Harris had made the horse go. He had reached over and picked up the leather reins that were right in front of me. Then he had said something to the horse and had shaken the reins across the horse's back. I stared at the reins and tried to think of the magic word that made the horse run. The word came back to me.

"Giddyup!" I heard myself say.

I didn't mean to say it out loud, and I didn't think the horse would pay any attention to a little boy like me. I just wanted to try to do what Uncle Harris had done. But the horse began to walk, and it was walking fast. It wasn't walking slowly like it had before when Uncle Harris had first said that word. It was nearly trotting already, the way it had on the road. I heard the sleigh's rails whispering over the snowy lawn and then we were up onto the road. I didn't know how to stop it.

Out on the road, I looked north to where the road disappeared at the horizon. A low bank of gray clouds sat there where the sky hung low over Lake Erie. *I'm going to the North Pole!* I thought. I imagined how cold it would be when I reached the pole. No one would be there. I could never get home. Maybe there would be polar bears.

Luckily, I didn't start to cry, because Uncle Harris came running up beside the sleigh and then past me, up to the horse. He grabbed the halter around the horse's head. "Whoa!" he yelled.

The horse stopped suddenly. I stopped looking toward the North Pole and looked at Uncle Harris. He wasn't mad, but he wasn't smiling either.

"Guess he wanted to take you for another ride," he said with a little laugh.

I nodded as Uncle Harris got up in the sleigh next to me. He pointed the horse and sleigh off the road into our orchard to turn around, and we were soon in front of the house again. It wasn't until he said "Whoa" again that I remembered what I was supposed to say to stop the horse.

"That was quite a ride!" Mama said with a little laugh as I got down from the sleigh.

"Anybody else want a ride?" Uncle Harris asked again.

"We have to get to town before the bank closes, Harris," Daddy said. "That's a great sleigh. Thanks for the rides for the boys."

Then Daddy looked at me and smiled. "Next time you might have a helper," he said to Uncle Harris.

I smiled a little and felt embarrassed but also a little proud. I had nearly been pulled to the North Pole by a runaway horse and sleigh that I couldn't stop, but I *had* driven a sleigh, almost like Santa Claus.

(A few farm horses were still in use in the mid-1940s at the time of this story, but in about five years, most of them were gone. Farmers then used tractors and trucks, so I never had a chance to drive a horse-drawn sleigh again.)

53
Dog and Boy Bike Crash

ONE SUNNY SUNDAY AFTERNOON while my dad was at work at the Sun Oil refinery in Toledo, I took my bike for a short ride down the road and went only as far as the next house, the Viebrooks' house. I had just learned to ride, and I was using the girl's bike my father had bought to make it easier for us three boys to learn to ride. I pedaled out for a short ride, and the air blew past my face like the wind.

The Viebrooks family had a loop drive, and I could practice bike riding by going around the loop without stopping. Their driveway was covered with black cinders from the kilns of the old Gleckler tile-making factory. The factory was gone, but the black cinders from the furnaces were still there on the driveway. The cinders had sharp edges, not like the white limestone gravel on the road.

I started to ride around the loop, but all of a sudden, a black blur came zooming from the house. It was barking and running right at me. I tried to swerve, but Johnny Viebrooks' dog ran right into my front tire. The bike reared up like a bucking horse, the dog yelped and rolled under the tire, I fell off the bike onto the black driveway, and the dog ran away.

The "girls' bike" that ran over the dog: Arlin Kardatzke with daughter Sharon and sons Owen and Nyle about three years before the accident.

My big brother Merl saw the crash and came running over. I stood up to wipe the dirt off my pants, but my brother said, "Sit down! Sit on the grass. Pull up your pant leg. Let's see if your knee is okay. You landed right on it."

I sat down on the grass and pulled up my right pant leg. It was okay. I pulled up the left pant leg. Yikes! There was a big, bloody gash right across my knee. It was the biggest cut I had ever seen. The cut went deep into my knee, and I could see some white stuff. I didn't know what the white stuff was, but it must have been my kneecap or a ligament or something that held my leg on. I just stared at it.

"Oh, no!" Merl yelled when he saw my leg. "You have a bad cut! I'm going to get Mama!"

He jumped on the bike and rode back to our house, yelling, "Mama! Mama! Help! Mama!"

It was Mama's Sunday afternoon nap time, but this was an emergency. Merl didn't know that our younger brother Owen had been yelling for our mother a little earlier. He had climbed high up in the cherry tree and wanted Mama to see how high he had climbed. He yelled and yelled until she got up from her nap and came outside to see him in the tree. She had just settled in again when Merl came yelling into the house.

"Nyle got hurt!" he said. "Nyle got hurt! He has a gash on his knee!"

My mother's irritation and her thought of a nap vanished. "Where is he?"

"He's over at Viebrooks' house. He ran over their dog on his bike and fell off. He's over there on the grass."

"I better go look," Mama said, rising from the bed.

Mama hurried around the pond toward me while Merl rode the bike on the road. I still had the leg straight and my pant leg rolled up when they got there. Mama looked at my knee.

"Oh! My goodness! How did it happen?" she said.

I told her how the dog had run in front of me and how I had fallen after I ran over it. She kept staring at my knee.

"We have to take you to the doctor," she said. "We better see if Grampa is at home. Merl, take the bike and go to Grampa's and see if he can come."

Merl hopped on the bike and pedaled out onto the road to Grampa's house as fast as he could go, and in a few minutes he came back.

"Grampa's coming! He's coming now!" he yelled, and just then Grampa's big black Buick pulled into the driveway. He stopped on the other side of the loop drive and came over to me. He looked at my knee and then at Mama. He raised his eyebrows.

"We better get him to the doctor," Mama said. "I think he may need stitches."

"Yep. Looks like it," Grampa said. "I kin take him to O'Karbor." (That's how Grampa and most people in Leatherport said "Oak Harbor.") The doctor that's working on Sundays is there today."

The doctor in Oak Harbor and the one in Elmore traded weekend duties. Our regular doctor was in Elmore, but all the doctoring business this weekend went to Oak Harbor, about eight miles away.

Grampa picked me up, and Mama opened the Buick's back door. Grampa put me down on the seat with my leg stretched out straight.

"Be okay there?" he asked me. I nodded and looked at my knee.

Mama sent Merl back to our house to take charge of my younger brother Owen and our four-year old sister Sharon, and she got in the front seat with Grampa.

At the doctor's house in Oak Harbor, we could see through the front window of his living room that he was playing cards with some people. Mama went to the front door and told him about my knee. The doctor wasn't happy to leave his card game, but he went downstairs to his office in his remodeled garage. He opened the door for us, and Mama helped me walk inside while I held my pant leg up out of the blood. Grampa went with us but stayed in the waiting room while we went into a small clinic room.

"Get up on that table and let me have a look," the doctor ordered, pointing to the examination table.

I sat on the edge of the examination table and turned so my leg stretched out straight on top of the table.

"Hmm," the doctor said. "Gotta stitch that up."

He brought a bottle of alcohol and a wiping pad and began swabbing my knee hard to get all the dirt out. The alcohol and his rubbing stung my knee. I winced and yelled, "Oww!"

The doctor turned and opened a little cabinet and worked on something there for a minute. He turned toward me with a curved needle and some thread. He spoke to Mama.

"Better hold that leg down so I can sew it up."

Mama held my leg down, and the doctor began to sew. He didn't give me a shot for the pain but just started sewing. Any numbness from the fall was gone, and the pain from the needle was awful. I screamed and cried.

"Stop!" I yelled. "Stop! It hurts too much!"

"Oh, you want me to stop?" the doctor asked gruffly. "Would you like it better if I cut your leg off!"

"Yes!" I yelled, but then I said, "No!"

Mama didn't say anything, so the doctor went back to work. He used little pliers to push the needle through the skin. After each stitch, he tied a knot in the thread and cut off the loose ends. He kept sewing until there were seven stitches across the huge cut. I kept yelling and crying as he sewed me up.

When he finished sewing, he put more alcohol on the stitched leg and wrapped my knee in a big, white bandage that went all the way around my knee several times.

"There. That'll hold it. Better bring him back in a week to have the stitches out. That'll be five dollars," the doctor said matter-of-factly.

Mama fished in her purse for the money and helped me off the exam table. "Do you think you can walk to the car?" she asked.

"I think so," I said and began a stiff-legged walk to the waiting room. I didn't have to worry anymore about getting blood on my pants. I looked up at Grampa. He wasn't smiling. He wasn't smiling *at all*. His face was red, and his eyes even seemed bigger than usual.

"You ready to go home?" Grampa said, looking at me.

He said it nicely. I could tell he was mad about something. I didn't know it then, but Grampa had overheard everything the doctor had said and how he had said it. Grampa was so angry he almost wanted to go in and fight the doctor. He probably thought the doctor should have given me a shot to stop the pain, and he should have at least talked nicer.

Grampa and Mama helped me into the back seat again with my leg out straight on the seat. They talked quietly in the front seat as we pulled out onto the main street into downtown Oak Harbor. Grampa stopped the car in the middle of town and went into a store. He came back with a big bag of colorful hard candy and opened the car door beside me.

"Here you go," he said as he handed me the candy. "Hope this will help."

My eyes must have been wide. I had never seen such a big bag of candy before. I said thanks to Grampa, and he got back into the car to drive us home. Mama thanked Grampa too. I looked at the bag of candy all the way home, and my brothers and I had some that afternoon. I was okay the rest of that Sunday, and I went to school the next day.

The kids on the school bus saw the big bandage on my knee and heard that I had stitches. Johnny Viebrooks had told them.

"My dog wrecked Nyle's bike, and he got his leg cut. He ran over my dog, but my dog is okay."

My leg healed quickly, and when a week had passed, my mother looked at the stitches as she washed my knee. She had been thinking about that doctor in Oak Harbor and that he had said to bring me back so he could take out the stitches.

"I think I can take those stitches out myself," Mama said. "Do you want me to try?"

I thought about the doctor too. "Okay," I said, not wanting to go back to the doctor for any reason.

Mama put alcohol on my knee like the doctor had done, but she did it gently, and my knee had healed so much that the alcohol didn't sting. With her sewing scissors, she snipped one of the stitches and used tweezers to pull it through the skin and out. It didn't hurt, but I could feel it sliding out. It almost tickled.

"How was that?" Mama asked.

"Okay," I said. "It didn't hurt."

Mama went ahead and pulled out all the stitches, and she put more alcohol on my knee. I wanted her to keep the stitches so I could show them to other kids, but she threw them away.

My knee healed completely, but the big scar stayed there. Whenever I went swimming in cold water, I could see the scar better than any other time. For a long time the scar was pale purple when I got cold.

When I went to Africa in the Peace Corps as a young man, the people in charge asked if I had any scars that would identify my body in case I died in an accident. I told them about the scar on my knee, but I didn't die in Africa, so nobody had to use the scar identify my body.

(As a young boy, I thought the name of Oak Harbor was "O'Karbor," like an Irish name. When I learned to read maps, I didn't tell anybody what I had thought before. This is the first time I have told anyone the whole story about running into the dog and getting the scar. I almost never look at it now, and nobody seems to want to see it.)

Part Eight

Elmore, a City on a Hill

54
The Town of Elmore

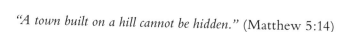

"A town built on a hill cannot be hidden." (Matthew 5:14)

"For we must consider that we shall be as a city upon a hill."
(John Winthrop, 1630)

ELMORE MAY NOT HAVE BEEN the "town built on a hill" mentioned in the Bible or John Winthrop's "city upon a hill," but it was a center of life for the people of Leatherport and Harris Township. At Christmas, Elmore seemed like Bethlehem, and on the Fourth of July, it became Ft. McHenry. In its devotion to America and our institutions of freedom and responsibility, Elmore was like Winthrop's city on a hill.

Elmore's bright lights at night were not visible in downtown Leatherport, but it was comforting to know that the lights were on in Elmore. It was the town closest to Leatherport, and people relied on it for their many business, educational, and religious needs. Elmore's stores sold groceries, fresh meat, medicine, hardware, clothing, and even jewelry until Walmart and other big-box stores took over.

The downtown Elmore business district today looks a lot like its pictures from the 1880s. Flat storefronts line the block-long row of shops. Google Maps reveals that nearly all the roofs on Rice Street are flat, but in earlier times, the raised storefronts concealed peaked roofs and made buildings look grander than they were.

Notable buildings in Elmore were the meat store, the food locker, the ice plant, two restaurants, the bank, and the general store. Each has its memorable story or two along with other stories of Elmore town.

(The expression "a city on a hill" has appeared often in American political oratory. John Winthrop used it in his charge to the Massachusetts Bay colonists before they left on their voyage to Boston in 1630. It has become an appeal to American exceptionalism.)

55
The Elmore Library

As the cultural center of Harris Township and the Leatherport area, Elmore needed a library, but no Elmore Library existed until long after Leatherport had disappeared and had become a fading memory. No library was known in Leatherport, but the Leatherport School had books, including McGuffey Readers, arithmetic books, and simple history books. The earliest thoughts of a local library arose to the southwest of Leatherport, in Elmore.

To be a cultural center, Elmore needed a library. An active library association existed in Elmore in 1886, but not until 1892 did residents try to establish a library. That plan didn't materialize immediately, and the idea lay dormant for another forty-five years, until a plan arose again in 1937 to organize a public library in Elmore. It was 1945 before the Elmore Federation of Women's Clubs succeeded in opening a library. It was set up in lobby space at the Brandes and Trautman Food Locker on Toledo Street.

By 1952, the library had outgrown its Food Locker space and was moved to a room on the second floor of the Willard Weis law office on Rice Street. Within two years, that space, too, was filled with books. Dreams of a new, free-standing library began to circulate. A Library Board was established by the Town Council, and it worked for several years to develop plans and financing.

In the spring of 1959, construction began on the first parts of the current library building located directly across Clinton Street from the library's first home at the Food Locker. The new library was completed in 1960, and it has had several more additions and renovations over the years—in 1976, 1991, 2002, and 2019. The 2019 expansion was completed with funds mainly from local donors.

Besides books, the current library offers computer and internet access, audio and video materials, and exemplary local history research.

(The Grace Luebke Local History Collection in the Elmore Library was created through a lifetime of work by Grace Luebke [1920–2009]. It is a growing treasure trove of documents and pictures throwing light on the lives lived in and near Elmore from its earliest times to the present. Expert research assistance is available through dedicated staff. Parts of this book would have been impossible without research support from Katie Blum, the library's research assistant.)

56
Tank's Meats

TANK'S MEATS HAS BEEN family-owned and operated since 1907. It was once on Rice Street in downtown Elmore, but it is now just south of town on Route 51, at the Ohio Turnpike entrance. Tank's Meats is a travel destination for those of us who know of it, and its location on the turnpike makes it easy to reach. Fresh meat and a dazzling array of sausages and lunch meats are there, along with a collection of spices and other foods to be found only at Tank's.

Visitors to Tank's can buy "Tank's Meats" sweatshirts and t-shirts right at the checkout counter. I wear my Tank's shirts around Indianapolis, and I'm sure some people here envy me. On trips to Elmore, I have often filled an ice chest with Tank's meats to "smuggle" across the state line to my home in Indiana. Other shoppers, I'm told, have carted off Tank's meats to as far away as Texas and Colorado.

Leatherport, Ohio

Until a few years ago, the Tank's slaughterhouse was right behind the store. Its location made it possible, if the owners chose, to slay a steer there in the morning and have its roasts and steaks on sale that afternoon. Nothing says freshness like beef from Tank's Meats that was on the hoof a few hours earlier.

57
The Food Lockers

―――――✦✦✦―――――

ON A HOT, HUMID SUMMER AFTERNOON, it was a pleasure to go to the food locker building in town with Mama and be greeted by Kenny Damschroder, the affable proprietor. Walking into the locker area was like a blast of winter on the hottest summer days, and it made us appreciate summer even more. After a few minutes of bone-chilling cold inside, the heat and humidity outside felt good for a few minutes.

The hallway inside Elmore's food locker building was lined with locker drawers stacked from floor to ceiling, like vaults in a morgue or in the mausoleum in a cemetery. People who had a numbered key could walk right into that frigid storage building whenever they needed to. They could pull something out of their locker for dinner, or they could deposit vegetables or strawberries from their gardens. Lockers provided much-needed storage for large farm families. It was common for people to freeze a quarter or half a steer at butchering time.

Leatherport, Ohio

The food locker building and the ice plant in Elmore replaced the old icehouse out on Graytown Road. Electricity produced ice better than the winter cold and the ponds, and it made ice all year. Electricity eventually became available to every home, and refrigerators and freezers replaced the need for ice and storage space in town.

The food locker building in Elmore was across Clinton Street from where the Elmore Library now stands and diagonally across from the Masonic Lodge. I "flew over" the place on Google Maps recently and discovered a start-up church where the lockers once operated. It's surely a warmer place now.

(The food locker building is now called "The Block" and is the youth outreach program for the Bethel Church two miles east of town.)

58
The Ice Plant and Ice Cream

━━━━━━━◆◆◆━━━━━━━

ON SUNDAYS WHEN WE PLANNED TO churn ice cream after dinner, we stopped at the Kuhlman ice plant on Fremont Street in Elmore for a huge block of ice. The older Mr. Kuhlman would come from his house to the small loading dock next to the small building where the ice was made and stored.

We kids loved to see Mr. Kuhlman bring out a gleaming 50-pound block of ice. He carried it to us with ice tongs that bit into the ice on both sides. We kids had to raise our feet up high so he could slide the block of ice into the back seat in front of us. We soon took off our shoes and socks and froze our feet all the way home.

Picking up the ice after church was the easy part. The hard part came in the afternoon. First the ice had to be broken into small enough pieces to fit into the ice cream freezer. It was not easy. Daddy hoisted the big block of ice into a burlap bag and laid it on the concrete walk behind our house. He brought out the special mallet that had no other purpose than pulverizing ice for ice cream. The mallet was made from part of a big apple tree limb. The wooden handle was about eight inches long, and the mallet head was about seven inches in diameter. It took a strong man or a very strong kid to swing that mallet and break the ice. Using the ice mallet become a rite of passage for maturing kids.

When the block of ice had been hammered into small pieces, Mama brought out the ice cream canister filled with cream, sugar, and vanilla. She placed it carefully in the ice cream freezer bucket and clamped on the freezer's top, taking care to see that its gears fit exactly right on the top of the canister. A metal grid (called the paddle) inside the canister would stir the ice cream when someone cranked the freezer. All the helpers grabbed handfuls of ice and packed it between the canister and the sides of the wooden bucket. They added salt as each layer of ice went in, and more salt was spread across the top. The salt made the ice melt faster, and the faster it melted the more heat it absorbed from the ice cream. A small rug or a folded bag on top kept the freezer cold as it was being churned.

Churning the ice cream was easy at first, but as the cream thickened into ice cream, turning the crank became harder and harder. Near the end, one of the bigger kids or my dad had to take over, cranking until the crank couldn't be moved. At last the ice cream was ready!

Someone lifted the canister and took it to the kitchen. It was supposed to sit for an hour or two in the bucket to harden fully, but the workers usually were too hungry to wait. Soft, soupy ice cream was ladled out, and one lucky person was allowed to lick the "paddle" that had stirred the ice cream so well. It was a great way for grown-ups and kids to celebrate a summer Sunday afternoon.

(Making ice cream like this may be a genetic trait in my family. We always made a freezer of ice cream when relatives came from out of state. It's possible that the ice cream habit came with our ancestors from Germany.)

59
Hardware Stores in Elmore and the Big Fire

───────✣───────

THE ELMORE HARDWARE STORES KEPT farms, homes, and businesses operating for many years. If Google Maps is to be believed, there is no longer a hardware store in Elmore. If true, wrack, ruin, and devastation could be just around the corner. A town could hardly survive without at least one hardware store. Maybe a store in a nearby town is keeping Elmore in good repair, or maybe Elmorites must travel to Toledo for tools, paint, and nails.

There were two hardware stores in Elmore in the 1940s, Jaeger Hardware and the Elmore Hardware. These undoubtedly were bulwarks of home, building, and machine upkeep, but I have only inconsequential memories of them.

My earliest hardware store memory is from Christmas 1946 when I had just turned seven. I was with my dad on an errand at Elmore Hardware when it was on Toledo Street near the food lockers. Next to the door was a display of Christmas wreathes with holly leaves made of colorful red and green foil. A backing ring of pasteboard held the leaves and an electric candle together. My family didn't have a wreath at home, but I somehow knew what it was at my tender age. I was overjoyed when Daddy bought the wreath, and it may still be with my Christmas decorations here in my house … somewhere.

Another hardware store memory is from the Jaeger Hardware, on the north side of Rice Street near Neeb's Garage. I bought my first gun there when I was eight years old. My dad was against guns of any kind, especially for young boys, but I kept asking if I could have a BB gun. He finally agreed I could buy one if I saved my own money for it. He probably thought I could never raise that much money because I was a well-known spendthrift. But my passion for a BB gun was so powerful that I suppressed my spending impulses until I had amassed the $5.00 price of a Red Ryder lever-cocking BB gun.

(Neeb's Garage was owned by the Neeb family. An elderly Neeb aunt had come from Germany in the early 1900s and was one of the first to see a newborn Neeb baby. In her German accent she exclaimed, "He looks yust like a nape!" That sounded like, "He looks just like an ape!" She actually said, "He looks just like a Neeb!" Her approval of the child "went viral" before viral existed.)

(An online price level calculator says that $5.00 was the equivalent of $53.92 in 2020 money. You can buy the same BB gun at Walmart now for $29.26, but I'm not telling you to actually buy a BB gun.)

My dad's face must have fallen when I shared the wonderful news that I had saved $5.00. He drove me to town and parked directly across from the Jaeger Hardware store. While still in the car, he asked me to think of anything else I might want to buy with the $5.00. I didn't really try. My wandering little mind had focused on a BB gun, and nothing could take its place. Daddy reluctantly went across the street with me and assured the store owner that my purchase was parent-approved, even if he wished it wasn't happening. I bought the BB gun and two small tubes of BBs, the first of thousands of BBs I shot all over northern Leatherport.

I shot that BB gun around the ponds often. Many frogs, birds, and large bugs suffered. I became a dead shot and could hit small objects at thirty paces just holding the gun at my waist. Alas, the BB gun's spring eventually tired and the cocking mechanism failed. I chose to retire it.

(*That precious BB gun is still in my basement here in Indianapolis, and it may end up buried or cremated with my body.*)

The third hardware store memory is from the day Elmore Hardware Store went up in flames in April 1955. I was in high school and was with a few other Future Farmers of America at Danny Woods' house on Route 51 when the fire broke out. We were shoveling chicken manure into a trailer (some of the boys had less polite terms for our cargo). We were going to scatter it on our Vocational Agriculture field on the east side of Elmore. Someone looked up and saw a tower of black smoke rising above Elmore. We stopped shoveling and gaped at the smoke.

"Let's go!" one of the boys yelled.

We didn't need to hear more. The fire stopped all shoveling of chicken droppings that day. We jumped into cars and drove as close as we could get to the fire.

The Elmore Hardware was a total ruin, but soon after the fire there was a huge sale. Water-damaged goods were sold at a deep discount. The greatest treasure I carted off was several boxes of 20-gauge shotgun shells. The paper boxes had faded in water during the fire, but the shells all worked in my old shotgun. The shotgun went off with a wonderful roar when I pulled the trigger, but it killed fewer of God's creatures than my Red Ryder BB gun.

The Elmore Hardware was reopened on Rice Street, but it never had the drama of its smoldering, dripping wet forebear. The Jaeger Hardware is gone, but I don't know the details of its demise.

Elmore hardware fire, 1955.

(This aerial photo of the hardware store fire is from the Elmore Library website. Doug Pickard, a member of the Class of 1957, was an avid photographer with a better camera than anyone else in the class could have imagined. He somehow hitched a plane ride with Paul Haar, the proprietor of Haar International Airport, a grass landing strip east of Elmore. You can see more than one marvelous aerial picture of the 1955 fire by searching for "Hardware Fire" on the Elmore Library website.)

60
Chasing the Fire Truck

"BACK IN THE DAY," fires near Elmore were among the greatest forms of excitement after the War. When the fire siren sounded on the water tower high above Elmore, volunteer firemen dropped their work wherever they were and hurried to the firehouse. At the firehouse, they suited up for action and headed out to the fire. Some had phones in their homes or businesses and called to learn their destination so they could meet the engine there.

The fire might be in a barn or a house, or it might be in a field of dry grass, or there might have been a car fire or a terrible wreck. Whatever the emergency, people in town wanted to know about it. Some wanted to get to the fire as fast as the firemen. Like the trained volunteer firemen, the "volunteer witnesses" dropped everything, raced to town, and followed the fire truck.

The fire truck, its siren wailing, led a parade of cars, trucks, and an occasional motorcycle. It was an awesome sight. There must have been legitimate firemen in the line of vehicles, but most of the drivers seemed to be eager gawkers. Winding along a country road, the colorful procession looked almost like a religious procession from the Middle Ages.

It may be illegal to chase a fire truck now in the twenty-first century, even if you are out in the country near Leatherport. You're not likely to see a posse following the modern fire trucks. Chasing the fire truck, or seeing the truck's entourage, is just one of the things you have missed by being born at the wrong time and the wrong place, not in Elmore in the middle of the twentieth century.

61
The Portage Inn

THE PORTAGE INN MAY BE THE oldest continuously operating restaurant in Elmore. It always seemed popular, and I had the impression there was something special about the food there.

The Portage Inn served liquor, so my family didn't go there because we didn't go to places that served alcohol. The only kind of alcohol my parents approved was the rubbing alcohol we put on cuts at home. The taste of rubbing alcohol was so nasty we kids wondered why anyone would want to drink it. Our church was against alcoholic drink, and we believed the church was right.

A common word back then to label a person who never drank alcohol was *teetotaler*. All my family members were "teetotalers." We thought anyone who drank alcohol was in danger of becoming a "drunkard," but we knew very few who came close to that.

62
Hartman's Lunch and the Village Inn

———◆◆———

THE VILLAGE INN OFFERS A variety of dishes, including a fish fry every Friday. The featured fish are little perch that presumably were swimming in the clear waters of Lake Erie on Thursday. There's no way to count the number of Lake Erie perch that have been at the Village Inn for dinner. On other days, the menu can satisfy the appetite of the hungriest farmer or trucker.

At the Village Inn you will notice a large round table, and it's usually occupied by a group of men who look as though they could comprise the jury in a trial. Or maybe they are the spiritual descendants of King Arthur's Knights of the Roundtable.

Leatherport, Ohio

Before there was a Village Inn, there was Hartman's Lunch at the same location. If Hartman's menu exists anywhere, it must be in the archives of the Elmore Library.

63
Delivering Milk in Elmore

———✥———

FOR SEVERAL WEEKS I HAD A Saturday morning job as the assistant to Eli the Milkman. If I ever knew his last name, I have forgotten it. I may have been fifteen years old when I had the job.

Eli delivered milk to our house after Grampa died and we no longer could get fresh milk from him. Eli came in the dark hours of the morning on Saturdays, shortly after 5:00 a.m. We never locked the house in those days, so he set the milk inside the back door. He was there and gone in two minutes.

I had to get up very early one Saturday morning to apply for the job. Eli may have wanted company on his gloomy milk route, or he may have wanted to train someone to make some of the many drop-offs at houses and businesses in Elmore. After a brief conversation, I was hired. He said I could start the next Saturday.

Leatherport, Ohio

Saturday came around, and I somehow was ready at 5:00 a.m. for my first day on the job. It was winter, so it was dark and there was no hope for light for at least two hours. The cold was like that in a Siberian labor camp, but I was exhilarated to have a job. Eli and I made halting conversation on the way to Elmore, and we began stopping to leave milk at houses unfamiliar to me as a country boy. Eli knew what each customer wanted, and he put the right number of glass bottles into a metal caged basket. I could carry as many as six or eight bottles, but I was happier with little deliveries of one or two.

As dawn was breaking, we drove slowly down the back alleys of downtown Elmore, both of them, and left crates of milk at the back doors of businesses. Some of the crates were so heavy that Eli himself had to trundle them to the back doors. Most of the businesses were still closed, but there was a little store on the edge of town with the lights on. Eli went inside and made that delivery himself and was warmly greeted by the lady in charge.

I got off work about 11:30 a.m., and one of my parents picked me up in town. Eli paid me a few dollars. I was thrilled to have earned some of my own money at my age.

The thrill of milk delivery wore off after a couple of months. It was hard to get up so early, and I began to guess that the money wasn't worth it. I finally came to my senses and told Eli one morning that I wouldn't be going with him anymore. He seemed mildly disappointed, but I was relieved. No more 5:00 a.m. morning wake-ups for me.

64
The Bank of Elmore

The most formal institution in Elmore was The Bank of Elmore. I never put much money in the bank, probably because I rarely had more than $50. As a kid, my main pleasures at the bank were the heavy door on the vault and the free scales where I weighed my skinny body.

The vault door was always open when my family visited on Saturday mornings. We could look inside at the shiny metal boxes where people stored who-knows-what. We didn't know what might be stored in them because we didn't have a box, and nobody we knew had one. Still, just the look of the vault door was awe-inspiring.

The vault door must have made people feel their money was safe in the bank. Feeling confident that the vault was safe was probably more important than the fact that a blast of dynamite couldn't have opened the vault. Heavy stainless steel rods in the door reached into the steel frame when the door was closed.

Leatherport, Ohio

The free scales were of more practical interest to me. I weighed myself every time I went to the Bank of Elmore with my parents as a young kid and even later when I was a teenager and once as an adult. Now I would pay money to be weighed again and see the same numbers I saw on the bank scale back then.

(Even though the Bank of Elmore is long gone, I suspect the same massive vault door is still there in the beautiful stone building now occupied by the Commodore Perry Federal Credit Union.)

65
Damschroder's Store

THE MOST NOTABLE OF ALL BUILDINGS in Elmore was Damschroder's Store, opened in 1864 by C.H. Damschroder. My great-grandparents shopped there in the 1890s, and every generation of Elmorites shopped there for decades.

Damschroder's had been a general store in the 1800s with groceries and tools alongside racks of clothing and collections of shoes and boots. By the 1950s, it had become the Damschroder Dry Goods Store, but it no longer sold groceries and tools. It was still a good place for clothes, especially winter coats. By the 1980s, Damschroder's was mainly a dry goods and clothing store.

It may have been in the 1970s when I visited and noticed that Damschroder's still had old toys for sale. Some were from the 1940s, just after World War II. A small metal flute was labeled "Made in Occupied Japan." Small cars and airplanes made of thin metal seemed to be from the same period. The store carried the toys at very, very low prices. Some old toys were priced at ten cents each. By the 1970s some of the toys were antiques.

"Do you think you could ask higher prices for these toys?" I asked the lady behind the counter on one visit.

"No. That's what we paid for them, so we sell them that way," she explained.

I felt a little guilty, but I went ahead and bought a few toys. I wonder what they are worth today.

Damschroder's became an antique store, and about 1993, it became the Elmore 5 and 10 store. It operated under that name until the early 2000s. In 2017 it became the Elmore General Store, LLC, but it retained the "Elmore 5¢ and 10¢" sign above the door from its earlier incarnation. The online pictures now show an attractive, thriving store filled with quaint-looking reproductions of old-style crockery, gifts, candy, jam, and the work of local craftspeople. The gleaming hardwood floor does honor to the store's ancient heritage.

One vivid memory of Damschroder's remains a part of my heritage. The wife of a new minister in Elmore was shocked and indignant when my mother told her in glowing terms about Damschroder's store. Where the minister's wife came from, there had been a family of Schroders but no "damn Schroder's." My mother quickly cleared up her misunderstanding, and her explanation became part of Elmore's oral history. The minister's wife was soon happily reconciled to the wonderful world of Damschroder's.

66
The First Bermuda Shorts

PEOPLE LINED THE SIDEWALKS of Rice Street, Elmore's "main drag," for parades in the 1950s, or they did at least once. My family went to parades, but we were conservative in many ways, including the clothing we wore. We saw things in town parades that we never saw in Leatherport.

Once I saw a grown man wearing pants that came down below his knees but not to his ankles. He looked strange. No one teased him or made fun of him, but the few people who greeted him seemed cautious about it. After all, who would want to be seen talking with a *man* who wore *short pants* in public?

67
Saturday Night
Merchants' Drawings

———✦———

IN THE 1940s, MERCHANTS IN Elmore gave customers tickets like those you bought to enter a movie theater. Each ticket represented twenty-five cents spent in a store. Twenty-five cents at that time could buy two hamburgers or a dozen eggs, so don't sniff at it. Two dollars might buy a whole bag of groceries. The tickets were your reward for being a loyal Elmore shopper, and they could win you a prize at the weekly merchants' drawings.

To enter the drawings, people wrote their names on the backs of the tickets and tossed them into a jar or box in the store. Each week on Saturday, the signed tickets were rounded up from all the stores for the Saturday Night Merchants' Drawing.

People from town and the farms all around came for the Saturday night drawings. The drawings were held on the north side of Rice Street, right in front of George Brandow's insurance office in downtown Elmore and the bank next door. A farm trailer was the stage. A man stood on the stage and acted almost like an auctioneer, though it wasn't an auction. The man didn't chant like an auctioneer. He was more like a master of ceremonies for a big event, and he kept up a running, one-sided conversation with the crowd. He threw out jokes and funny comments to attract a crowd, and if he recognized someone in the crowd, he would call them out by name and introduce them. "Hey Earl!" he might yell to a friendly farmer, or "Lucille, you're looking lovely tonight!"

In front of the master of ceremonies was a barrel-shaped wire mesh container. Inside it people could see the merchants' tickets, including their own, and it looked like hundreds of tickets.

Before the drawing began, the MC on the trailer would throw handfuls of candy and bubble gum to the kids in the crowd. The kids all screamed and clamored for treats. Few things bring more joy to kids than free candy and bubble gum. The uproar attracted adults to the drawing, especially the kids' parents.

When my family went to the drawings, I usually stood in front of men who were standing on the curb a few feet from the drawing trailer. The men were tall, and they looked especially tall up there on the curb when I was just a kid down on the street.

Some of the men smoked cigarettes, and the smoke was like perfume to a non-smoker like me. Some men may have smoked pipes, but the most impressive smokers were those who smoked big, thick, black or brown cigars with smoke that could bring tears to your eyes. In the evening darkness, the sudden glow at the end of a cigarette or cigar looked as welcoming to me as a glowing fireplace. My family was against smoking, so being at the drawings was one of my earliest encounters with such sinful but appealing ways of the world.

Small kids like me needed to be careful around some of the men who weren't smoking. Those particular non-smokers had bulging cheeks and were chewing something that seemed as large as a handful of raisins. But they weren't chewing raisins; they were chewing huge wads of tobacco.

Every few minutes, each of the chewers would bow forward slightly. A thick, brown stream would spurt from his mouth and splatter on the street near his feet. This brown stuff was known as "tobacco juice." Women especially despised it, even more than they despised smoking. Kids near the chewers tried to avoid being showered with tobacco juice. This form of sin was far less appealing to me than cigarettes and cigars, but I sometimes chewed a wad of raisins at home and pretended it was chewing tobacco. I never spit out the delicious raisin juice, not even outside the house.

When it was time for the drawing, the man on the trailer yelled like an auctioneer and turned the cage full of tickets, keeping up his prattle the whole time. When he stopped the ticket cage, he opened a little door on the cage, reached in, and pulled out the first ticket. He looked closely to read the name scrawled on the ticket and then grandly announced the name. You would think he was introducing the President of the United States when he announced each name: "*Mrs.* Carl Anstead!" he might shout or "*Mr.* Johnny Hovis!" If a young kid's name was called, he might say something like, "Tom *Dolph!* A future mayor of Elmore!"

To win, you had to be there and come forward to get the prize, and cheers went up if the person was there. If no one came, another ticket was drawn. The winners were sometimes timid town people or farmers who weren't used to being famous. Those people seemed embarrassed and didn't hope for applause when their names were drawn. But the winner was sometimes bold and glad to have publicity and would make a great show of claiming the prize, waving it in the air after claiming it. That was always part of the fun.

The drawing continued until all the prizes and gift certificates had been handed over to the lucky winners. The crowd slipped away into the night. Parents claimed their children, and the men with cigarettes and cigars went home for one more smoke. Tobacco juice from the non-smokers stayed on the street until the next rain.

(These drawings were not gambling; if they had been, my conservative family would not have participated. You got your tickets just for buying something, and you didn't even have to hope *for a prize.)*

68
The Funeral Home

IF YOU LIVED NEAR ELMORE, "the funeral home" meant only one place. It was in the home of Fred and Elizabeth Sabroske, a great-uncle and great-aunt of mine. The home had been built as an attractive private home, but Fred and Lizzie Sabroske adapted it to serve funeral purposes as well.

The front door opened into an enclosed porch and then into the living room, which served as the main reception room for viewings. A small addition on the north side of the house was large enough for a casket and little more.

When visitors entered the house to see a body, they entered a quiet and reverent place. They spoke in hushed tones as they gazed at the carefully embalmed body. They shared memories of that person in life and sometimes talked of the hereafter. Carpet and upholstered furniture absorbed all sound that might otherwise have intruded on the serene atmosphere.

The house itself was always tidy and well-decorated when a body was shown, and it seemed it must have always been that orderly, just awaiting the next body of a departed person. The funeral home's tidiness seemed to create a feeling that the departed had led an orderly, meaningful life, even if the house oversold that impression in some cases.

An unwritten but often repeated ceremony was followed at every viewing. Visitors signed the guest book at the door. If they had brought a sympathy card or a memorial donation, there was a place to deposit them. Everyone greeted the others there, whether they knew them or not. Everyone spent at least a few moments silently gazing at the departed one. The funeral service itself was either in the funeral home or in a church. Some viewings and the funerals themselves were held in the home of the deceased.

In those days, visitors came to a viewing or a funeral in their best clothing. They didn't have to wear black, but it was understood that viewings and funerals, like weddings, were times for dress-up attire. The dignity of the occasions required it.

(The house that once served as the funeral home is across the street from the fire house at 235 Ottawa Street. Please do not disturb the current occupants.)

69
The Sabroske and Myers Furniture Store

BEFORE SHOPPING CENTERS AND massive all-purpose stores took over so much retail business, small towns were home to a wide array of stores. In Elmore there was a fine furniture store operated by the two men who ran the funeral home. Fred Sabroske and Richard Myers, the owners, were both licensed embalmers, but they also ran the furniture store in the middle of the main block in Elmore.

Entering the store was a little like going to the funeral home because of its quiet, impressive, adult atmosphere. It was so adult that I remember little about it. I left Elmore as a callow boy of seventeen when my furniture-buying days were decades in the future. On my few visits to the store, I quickly realized that the store was for more mature people with more money than I could even imagine as a high school student.

70
Elmore's Churches

IN 1951, THE SMALL TOWN OF Elmore may have seemed to some residents and visitors to match their mental images of a medieval European village. Residential streets were shaded by towering maple and oak trees, and several streets were paved with locally-fired paving bricks. The splendor of Christmas décor lit up the town in December while the town filled up with noise-muffling snow.

Most residents were no more than three generations from their first ancestors from the Old World. German was spoken by a few older people, and more than a few local customs had the flavor the Old World. The town's churches were an essential part of everyday life and the town's Old-World flavor.

The town was not dominated by a single church, as European villages might have been before the Protestant Reformation, but churches were a prominent part of Elmore. Newell Witte's 1951 history of Elmore listed seven churches within the town: Church of Christ, Church of God, Grace Lutheran Church, St. John's Evangelical and Reformed Church, St. Paul's Methodist Church, Trinity Lutheran Church, and Trinity Methodist Church.

The Hall Road Church was two miles east of town, and neighboring towns offered more ecclesiastical options. There once had been a Catholic Church at the corner of Rice and Congress Streets, next door to the present Church of God. Pointed window peaks make the former church easy to spot even today. After it closed its doors, Catholic believers were served by a church in Genoa and those in other nearby cities.

My immediate family and many of our extended family members attended the Church of God. I have shared stories and details about our church in a previous book, *The Clock of the Covenant.*

Church life remains important in Elmore, even as secular distractions seem to intrude more than in the mid-1900s.

71
Elmore's Centennial Celebration

---✤---

In 1951, Elmore celebrated its 100-year anniversary. Banners and signs proclaimed Elmore's importance, and special events were held all summer. There was a carnival with tents and scary rides and games where kids could win toys and little plaster dolls. There was a balloon ascension at the school, where a man in a basket went skyward under a hot air balloon.

The balloon ascension was not like one you might see today when hot air balloons take off, fly, and land routinely. The hot air for today's balloons is from gas-burners that quickly and cleanly fill them with heated air. Instead, the hot air for the centennial balloon came from a smoky oil fire in a barrel. The hot, smoky air filled the canvas balloon, and it tugged the ropes held by volunteers on the ground.

At the right moment, the balloon pilot jumped into the basket. "Everybody let go!" he yelled, and up he went. When the balloon was high enough, he jumped from the basket and parachuted to the ground. The gaping viewers applauded his bravery and were glad the ascension hadn't ended in tragedy. The balloon cooled, collapsed, and fell into a nearby bean field.

The canoe race held on the Portage River on the Fourth of July spread Elmore's glory all the way to Oak Harbor. On the day of the race, eager paddlers put their canoes in at Elmore to paddle downstream on the Portage River to Oak Harbor about nine miles away. People gathered on the bluff above the river in Leatherport, at the end of Graytown Road, to see the marvelous flotilla round the bend.

Two muscular high school boys paddled the leading canoe, and they seemed like full-grown men to me. They were making good progress, but things inside their boat weren't going so well. They weren't experienced canoeists, so they had to constantly adjust their paddling. Just as they passed Leatherport, people could hear them arguing. One boy was yelling at the other boy about how to paddle. That boy yelled back, and then the first one yelled again. I blush even now when I remember the swearing I heard. I sometimes got mad at my brothers and yelled at them, but I sure wouldn't have wanted to have a bunch of strangers hearing me yelling, especially not during our town's centennial.

Other than that one incident, the centennial celebration was a huge success. Elmore is now more than halfway to its bi-centennial.

Part Nine

Toledo Stories

72
Toledo, Ohio

———✦———

THERE IS A CITY IN SPAIN called Toledo. It's pronounced "to-lay-do" in Spain, but historians agree it must be our Toledo's namesake, even though we say "to-lee-do." After all, the newspaper in our Toledo is called *The Toledo Blade,* and Toledo, Spain, is famous for its excellent swords. What better proof could there be?

Leatherport and Elmore existed in the shadow of Toledo, that great city to their north. While Leatherport and Elmore were farm villages, Toledo was a large, modern, industrial city. It towered over Leatherport as a great beacon of civilization, knowledge, and news.

My family knew the world news because Jim Uebelhart read the news each day at noon on Toledo's WSPD radio. We also heard the news from Detroit, Michigan, and from Windsor, Canada, just across Lake Erie. Grampa listened to the news on a big floor-model radio at noon each day. His radio had a deep bass sound that made the news sound especially historic.

Toledo's greatest claims to economic fame were the Willis–Ford–Overland car and jeep factory, the Libbey–Owens Glass Company, and three oil refineries, including Sun Oil. But kids were more attracted to other wonders in Toledo such as the zoo, an amusement park near the zoo, the high-level bridge across the Maumee River, and sightings of lake freighters at the wharves.

Toledo is sometimes known as the "glass capital of the world." Much credit for this label goes to the Libbey–Owens Glass Company, founded in 1818. The company made millions of tumblers, bottles, and lamp chimneys.

Toledo was a melting-pot city where people of many nationalities settled and mingled to form the city's unique character. In the mid-1900s some groups that had been in Toledo for generations still spoke their European languages and followed customs from the Old Country. "The Hungarian Hour" was broadcast on Sundays, and I listened to it on the car radio after church while we kids waited for our parents to finish talking. I felt almost Hungarian while listening to Hungarian music, but the most Hungarian thing about our family was the goulash my mother cooked, and it wasn't really Hungarian.

Sun Oil was the industry in Toledo that my family knew best. My father got a job there in 1941 just before the U.S. entered World War II. He worked there until 1971 and retired during the Vietnam War. Whenever we went to Toledo, my family's route into Toledo took us past the Sun Oil refinery, and the towering flame of the gas flare was one of our favorite sights.

The year before my father started at Sun Oil, there was a terrible explosion. Men had gone into a tall brick smokestack to complete a welding job. Gas had leaked into the stack and settled at the bottom. When the men lit their torch to weld, the gas exploded and blew out the bricks at the base of the stack. The bricks above collapsed onto the men. The collapse started a huge fire and created more explosions. Many men died and others were maimed.

Toledo, Ohio

When my dad started in 1941, he saw men with scarred faces and ears partially burned off. Other fires and explosions happened while he worked at Sun Oil, but overall it was a safe place, in spite of the hot oil and gasoline flowing through its steely veins.

73
Big-City Wonders

———◆———

DRIVING INTO DOWNTOWN TOLEDO, we crossed the mighty Maumee River on our version of the Golden Gate Bridge: the "high-level bridge," as we called it. That suspension bridge was majestic, and driving over it felt like flying. On lucky days we could see lake freighters at the docks below with their proud steering towers. Downtown Toledo looked especially dramatic and alluring from the high-level bridge. It was the biggest, grandest city we knew.

Department stores were the main reason my family went to downtown Toledo, usually for clothes or shoes. On those days, our destination was Tiedtke's, the Lion Store, or LaSalle and Koch's. The stores had huge plate glass display windows outside, and inside our senses were overwhelmed by what we saw, heard, smelled, and tasted. Christmas was an especially enchanting time. The stores were decorated extravagantly, and smells of pine trees, popcorn, and chocolate filled each store.

The shoe department in some of the stores had an especially interesting machine that let us look right through our shoes to the bones in our feet. The machine was called a fluoroscope, and we loved to look inside a new pair of shoes to see if our toes would have enough room to grow. If we tried on several pairs of shoes, we got to look at our feet each time through the magical machine.

The machine was actually an X-ray machine, which meant that we would have a 20-second blast of X-rays for every pair of shoes we tried on. In the mid-1950s, scientists realized the danger in overexposure to X-rays, and shoe-fitting fluoroscopes were taken out of stores. None of my family members or friends lost feet or toes due to X-ray exposure, but my older brother did have larger feet than the rest of us. He probably had his feet X-rayed more.

I was in my early teens when I had my first hot dog of the style most of us now call a Coney Island dog or a chili dog. The revolutionary experience took place at a small walk-up stand in downtown Toledo. My guide was my

Migrant housing across the pond.

friend Floyd Castello, whose family came to Ohio from Texas each year for migratory farm work. They spent summers in a migrant camp across the pond from our house, and Floyd was my summertime friend for three years.

Floyd was a little older than me, wore a tall pompadour hairdo, and had a flair for the dramatic in speech and dress. He could wear tropical "Florida" shirts that we self-conscious farm boys wouldn't have dared to wear in public or even at home. Floyd used to sing "Goodbye Joe, me gotta go, me-o-my-o, me gotta go and pole the pirogue down on the bayou" and "Wondering, wondering who's kissing you" and other romantic songs I might not have known without him.

In 1956, Floyd took me to a tiny hot dog stand near a streetcar stop in Toledo and helped me buy two hot dogs slathered with chili dog sauce and stacked high with chopped onions. It was wonderful. I had never tasted anything like it. I was thankful to have such a persuasive and worldly tutor as Floyd. The chili dogs were part of a small family business, and they were called Hungarian Hot Dogs back then. Tony Packo, the owner and founder, was the son of Hungarian immigrants, and he invented his inimitable hot dog sauce from Hungarian spices.

About two years after I had my first Hungarian Hot Dog with Floyd, I received a letter from one of Floyd's family members at their winter home in Texas. Floyd had been driving on a remote farm road where tall sugarcane blocked the view at an intersection, and there were no stop signs. Floyd's car was hit by another car, and he died at the scene of the accident. When his family returned in the spring to a migrant camp three miles away, I went to see them. We all wept together.

(On your next trip to Toledo, be sure to visit one of Tony Packo's cafes. Tony isn't there anymore, but his hot dogs and other delicacies are. You can also go online and buy the same delicious Tony Packo's hot dog sauce.)

74
The Toledo Zoo

TOLEDO'S MOST SPELLBINDING attraction was the zoo. Today it is far more modern and humane than the zoo my family knew in the 1940s. Back then we were comforted by the iron bars that kept the more dangerous critters confined. Lions and tigers breaking out on a dark night to ravage Toledo was a danger not to be trifled with. A ponderous elephant could have squashed us flat if it had broken out and had come to Leatherport. None did.

The elephants in the Toledo Zoo were fascinating. One day when I was about five, I watched an elephant shuffle thoughtfully around its cage. It had just squashed something flat under one foot. When it lifted that foot, there was a "cow pie" just the shape of its foot. This moment showed me something new. To my tiny mind, it revealed an amazing fact: Elephants poop out of the soles of their feet. It was on another trip to the zoo in a later year when I learned how they really do it.

On one visit to the zoo, I saw an especially wild monkey that delighted in throwing his feces at a man and woman standing in front of his cage, "feces" being a polite word for something else. When the monkey stopped throwing his stuff at the couple, it sat down directly in front of the couple. The man prepared to take a picture of the abusive critter, but the woman grabbed his arm.

"No!" she said. "Don't take a picture! His penis is showing!"

Sure enough, the monkey was rudely displaying his male monkeyhood, and the man put his camera away.

When my Aunt Ella and Uncle Silbert came to visit from Oklahoma with their kids, our combined families went to the zoo. There must have been nine kids in our troupe. It may have been the first zoo visit for the four young Oklahoma girls. When we came to the seal cage, the cousin my age yelled excitedly.

"I've seen those before! There's one in my coloring book!"

"What color did you make it?" her dad asked.

"Red!" she exclaimed proudly, and some of the grown-ups chuckled. My cousin had never seen a live seal and had chosen her favorite color.

I knew that was wrong. I had been to the zoo before.

Some things in the zoo were very, very puzzling. One was the fact that the polar bear seemed to always stand at the edge of her small concrete swimming pool, bobbing her head up and down without jumping in. On one visit, we waited a long time to see the polar bear jump in, but she didn't. We went on to see other creatures and went home.

Summer turned to fall, and fall turned to winter. Spring and summer came again. When school was out, we went to the zoo again. When we reached the polar bear cage, there she was, still bobbing her head up and down. I thought about the blizzards we'd had that winter, and I thought of the thick ice on our pond. I thought about the polar bear out there in the cold, bobbing her head all that time, maybe without eating or going to the bathroom. Even with its thick white fur, the polar bear seemed heroic. She somehow hadn't frozen while she stood there all winter bobbing her head. I had learned something amazing about polar bears, and it took me a long time to un-learn my belief that polar bears stand and bob their heads all year long.

I loved to see the snakes. My favorites were the colorful, venomous little snakes and the enormous pythons and boa constrictors. The big snakes were the fulfillment of the threat we saw in the garter snakes around the pond in Leatherport. The pythons spoke to me of power and horror and being squeezed to death. The snakes didn't speak in actual words like the one I'd heard about in the Bible story, but I got their messages anyway. If they had spoken, I might have fallen under their spell.

I must have been very young the day I misunderstood something important about the zoo and about my dad. I was at home leafing through a big black photo album. The pictures were black and white, like all other pictures at that time. I came to a picture of a big, cat-like animal lying inside the bars of an iron cage with long hair around its head and neck. The rest of its body was smooth, covered by only short hair. It had a long tail with a bundle of dark hair at the end. Its mighty paws were folded under its huge, menacing face. I stared with an open mouth. Just then Mama came rushing through the room on one of her motherly chores.

"What's this?" I asked her, pointing to the picture.

"That's when Daddy was in the zoo."

"That's when Daddy was in the zoo!" I repeated in my mind. Her answer explained a lot. I didn't know where daddies came from, and Mama had told me at last; daddies come from the zoo.

I looked again at the picture with new understanding. There Daddy was in his own cage, looking more beautiful and manlier than any of the other animals. He looked manly in a lionish way, and that was good to see. Even though he no longer looked like he did in that picture, there was still something lionishly strong about him.

When Daddy was a lion.

75
The Toledo Museum of Art

The Toledo Art Museum was as close as my family came to high culture in the 1950s. We made several trips there, and the effect was electric. I was a young boy, but a few sensational aspects of the museum remain in my memory to this day.

From the start, the mummies fascinated me. Those ancient, embalmed human bodies wrapped in burial cloth were the first thing I wanted to see on any museum visit. I would stand for minutes and stare at the mummies in their painted sarcophagi (the boxes they had been buried in) and dream of the ancient days before they died. The mummies fueled my interest in ancient Egypt. My Bible storybook had a picture of Moses being trained in Pharaoh's palace before he grew up and freed his people. Another picture showed Joseph handing out food to Egyptians during the famine. The mummified people in those boxes may have been in Egypt when Moses and Joseph were there. Maybe one of the mummies had known Joseph.

The art museum also boasted beautiful glass objects made by the Libbey Glass Company. My favorite thing from the Libbey Glass Company was a huge glass punch bowl. The museum may not have said so, but in my mind, it was the largest punch bowl in the world. At least it was the largest punch bowl in *my* world. If it were actually used for punch, I reasoned, it probably could hold twenty gallons of my favorite pink punch. Only pink punch would have done it justice.

The museum had a place called the Peristyle Theater for live shows. My mother went alone one dreary Sunday afternoon to see *The Messiah* performed there. The experience would have been too much culture for any of us kids at the time, but my mother returned to Leatherport inspired.

Much later in my cultural education, I discovered the museum's collection of Impressionist paintings. I had seen other Impressionist paintings in Paris, and they awakened me to what I hadn't appreciated at the Toledo museum. The paintings are amazing and enchanting, and the collection is larger than you might expect. Some of the paintings seemed to me as though they were painted near Leatherport, but of course they weren't.

Part Ten

War Stories

76
The Second World War

THE SECOND WORLD WAR STARTED a few months after my family moved to a brown rented farmhouse a mile and a half south of Graytown that we called simply "the brown house." World War II was just called "the war" while it was going on, and it was still called "the war" for many years after it ended. Other wars have come and gone since then, so you now must be specific if you want to talk about the Second World War. You can't just call it "the war."

America was in the war between 1941 and 1945. It was still raging in 1943 when my family moved two miles south from "the brown house" to the north edge of Leatherport. The war ended on Sunday, September 2, 1945, with Japan's surrender. My class, the graduating Class of 1957, entered first grade in Elmore two days later.

My parents both took jobs at the Sun Oil refinery in Toledo during the war. My dad became a permanent employee, repairing instruments that reported on flows of liquid and gaseous petroleum products as they were refined. My mother worked full-time in the refinery's laboratory for a year, testing the purity of oil products. Their jobs paid well and earned them enough to pay $2,700 to buy the pond house on two and a half acres of land in Leatherport. They paid off the house before the peace terms were signed.

The house next to the pond was a dazzling mansion to us kids, complete with electric lights, running water, and an indoor toilet. Many of the stories in this book took place in or near what I sometimes call the "Pond House." War prosperity gave my parents a house they could not have dreamed of owning otherwise.

(The Brown House Stories *is a book about childhood adventures that happened in our rented house near Graytown, Ohio. My family lived there from 1941 to 1943, before we moved to the house next to the pond.*)

77
Playing War and Crossing the English Channel

———————✠———————

THE WAR SEEMED FAR AWAY to my brothers and me. We knew very little about it while it lasted. My parents didn't talk about the war in front of us, and they didn't listen to the news on the radio when we might have heard it. They didn't want us kids to be caught up in thinking about the war or knowing much about it or being scared by it. Still, we sometimes tried to imagine what was going on.

My father was a pacifist at heart, even though he worked at the oil refinery and his work indirectly involved him in the war effort. My brothers and I were not allowed to "play war" or to have toy guns. Later, when we could have toy guns, we were told never to point them at anyone. My father broke my double-barreled popgun as a reminder of that rule when

I absentmindedly pointed it at him and pulled the trigger. I never did that again.

Three of my uncles were in the war, all of them in the Pacific Theater. Even after the war ended, I didn't know the danger my uncles had survived. To my naïve little mind their tours of duty in the Pacific seemed almost like vacation trips. Uncle Roz brought a coconut to my parents on one of his furlough visits, and the coconut seemed peaceful. Uncle Jim was in the Seabees, the Naval Construction Battalion that built landing fields for the island-hopping planes that moved the war in the Pacific toward Japan. He also helped build roads and wharves on conquered islands. As for my Uncle Paul, a bomber pilot, I learned much later that on one mission, the tail gunner was shot out of his plane. Uncle Paul was usually tight-lipped, and that helped him many years later as one of the highest officials in the Central Intelligence Agency. My mother couldn't resist asking him about his work. Uncle Paul never said, "I can't talk about that." He just smiled and changed the subject.

Two of my cousins had Army helmets and toy guns. They dug a fox-hole in their yard in Elmore, but I didn't know what a foxhole was. I just thought it was a hole in the ground to play in. No one was shooting at us, so I didn't get the point.

One sunny day in the summer of 1944, I learned something big about the war when some of the neighborhood kids were with us out on the big pond in the flat-bottom plywood boat my dad had built. Three of the older kids were talking about war news they had heard, including the D-Day invasion of June 6, 1944. They talked about real boats crossing a real English Channel. They didn't talk about how dangerous the invasion was for the invaders, and they probably didn't know. There was a path of open water through the tall cattails on the far side of the big pond, and the big kids steered us there. The older kids knew some geography and knew more about the war. One of them announced, "We're crossing the English Channel!" and named the path "The English Channel." The words made our pond sound impressive and important, even though I didn't have the faintest idea about the English Channel, let alone an invasion.

English Channel boys in 1947.

This was a few years after the real soldiers crossed the real English Channel.

78
The Wartime Train to Oklahoma

---※---

MY MOTHER WAS FROM OKLAHOMA. Her parents and most of her family were living there in 1945, so Mama took us three boys on the train for a visit in Oklahoma while Daddy stayed at home to work at Sun Oil. The train trip must have taken two days, maybe three. I was only five years old, so I remember only a few things, like the crowded passenger cars filled with soldiers.

I was sitting next to a window one afternoon as the train rounded a bend. My mother pointed out the window at the train's big, black engine and the tower of black smoke rising over the train. On straight track we couldn't see the engine, but there it was, going around the bend pulling our car and all the others. We could see only the coal car right behind the engine and a few passenger cars at the front of the train. The huge black engine and its cloud of smoke were the very image of power.

The windows of our passenger car were open most of the time since air conditioning barely existed then. Smoke from the engine and dust from the roadbed blew in the windows the entire time. When we reached Oklahoma, we must have been sweaty, dusty, and covered with soot. That didn't bother me, since I was just a kid. I'd had the magical experience of riding in a train full of soldiers, seeing the smoke from the engine, and traveling to the faraway place called Oklahoma.

79
Helping the Soldiers and Sailors

LATE IN THE WAR, maybe in November 1944, Mama and we three boys took a big burlap bag out to the deep ditch by the road in front of our house. Milkweeds had grown up along the ditch, and Mama had heard that the Navy needed the seed pods from milkweed to make life preservers for men whose ships sank in ocean water or whose planes crashed there. Milkweed seeds had silky, fluffy little parachutes that could make the sailors' life vests float, and the fluffy little milkweed parachutes would preserve their lives.

We kids and Mama gathered milkweed pods along the ditch and stuffed them into the burlap bag. Mama took the bag of pods to a collection place in Elmore the next day, and they were soon on their way into the war. We were glad we could help the sailors who were out in ships and airplanes fighting in the war.

We also helped in the war by praying for the soldiers and sailors every night at bedtime. Mama would read us a Bible story, and each of us would pray. We might pray about other things, too, but at the end of every prayer, we said, "And help the boys in the war."

80
Roosevelt's Death and the End of the War

WHEN PRESIDENT ROOSEVELT DIED in 1945, I was too young to know it had happened and what it meant. I hardly knew we *had* a president because I was only five years old. But the evening Roosevelt died, Grampa came in his black Buick to take our family on a drive into town. I think he felt it was such an important day that we should do something special. He may have wanted to give his grandchildren a way to remember the day.

My cousin Elaine was with us. Elaine was eight years old, just like my older brother Merl. Elaine seemed much older than eight when she said thoughtfully, "It's going to be strange saying 'President Truman' instead of saying 'President Roosevelt.'"

Merl must have known what she meant, because he said, "Uh huh."

I didn't know what she was talking about, so I kept quiet.

When Grampa drove us into Elmore, people were standing on the sidewalks in the rain. They just seemed to be there to see cars and trucks go by, but some were holding American flags. Many were dressed in black or had black strips of cloth around one arm.

Grampa made a couple of turns to take us past the small veterans' park across the street from the food lockers. The American flag there was only halfway up the pole, and my dad said, "See that? The flag is at half-staff. It's because of the president."

We looked, and the lowered flag seemed especially sad.

Grampa took our family on a drive into town on another important day, the day the war ended in Europe. That day, May 8, 1945, later was called "V-E Day" for "Victory in Europe." It was raining and dark when Grampa picked us up, but the good news had to be celebrated.

The town of Elmore never looked the way it did that night, either before or since. People were standing on the sidewalks on both sides of Rice Street in the rain. The school band was playing in front of the bank. People were yelling and clapping and laughing. Some were crying and wiping their eyes. Wads of newspaper and piles of confetti had landed in the street and looked like snowdrifts. We drove slowly through the block-long business area and circled around to see it again.

Grampa and Gramma didn't say much. Neither did Mama or Daddy. We boys were quiet too. Gramma and Grampa had seen the end of the First World War many years earlier. They knew what the end of a war meant.

The part of the war that was against Japan was still being fought in the Pacific Ocean when the war in Europe ended. Terrible battles were being fought on small islands, and American soldiers were dying on one beach after another or drowning while trying to reach the beaches. American military leaders thought there would be a million American casualties if they had to invade Japan itself. Even though V-E Day had happened, our nation was bracing for another bad year of war.

Three months later, our country dropped two atomic bombs on Japan. The first bomb was dropped on Hiroshima, Japan, on August 6.

On August9, another atomic bomb was dropped on Nagasaki, Japan. The American leaders made Japanese leaders believe that we had a lot more atomic bombs and could drop them any day.

On August 15, the Japanese emperor announced that Japan would surrender. Japanese leaders signed the surrender papers on the deck of the *USS Missouri* in Tokyo Bay on Monday, September 2, 1945. Because of the time difference between America and Japan, that day was September 3, 1945, in the United States. For kids in Leatherport and Elmore, that was an important day for another reason: the first day of school.

Tanks on Rice Street in Elmore celebrating the end of World War II.

81
Tattoos from Wartime

WHILE THE WAR WAS STILL GOING ON, I saw soldiers in their uniforms on the streets, in stores, and in church. When the war ended, millions of soldiers and sailors and pilots came home, and we still sometimes saw them in uniforms. We often saw the former soldiers in short-sleeve shirts and jeans or khaki pants, and they looked different from the men I knew in church or around Leatherport who hadn't fought in the war. Some of the returned soldiers had tattoos, but the local men did not.

As a young boy, I was interested in the pictures and words on the men's arms. When the men were swimming at the lake, I could see even more tattoos, the ones they had on their chests. I thought tattoos were just part of being in the war. I thought that by the time I grew up, nobody would have tattoos, at least no polite people. That's what I thought back then.

82
Preparing for the Next War

———◆◆———

ONE SUNDAY A FEW YEARS AFTER the war ended, I was out in the yard with Daddy when a noisy airplane began flying in circles and diving toward the earth over a farm field by our house. It looked like a warplane. We watched as the pilot made more loops, and I thought it looked like he was learning to fly in a war. It was a thrilling sight for me. But Daddy just looked up at the plane and shook his head and said, "He just wants to make war."

I thought Daddy probably was right. The man in the plane shouldn't be getting ready for another war. It was good that the war was over. Things were peaceful in Leatherport. I had lots to do like swimming, bike riding, and shooting my BB gun. I didn't want another war.

As I got older, we began to hear news about what happened after the war was over. We heard that people in Germany were starving. Some people from our church sent things to help them. We heard about the terrible deaths in Japan when the bombs were dropped, but we didn't know how to help. We heard about the people who had been killed in death camps in Europe, and we knew that was something the war had stopped.

Russia seemed to be worse than Germany and Japan, and we thought the Russians might start another war. I thought the Russians hated us and wanted to do mean things to us. I was mostly right. The Russians exploded an atomic bomb at a place called Semipalatinsk on August 29, 1949. The name of the place alone was frightening.

That news scared me. In my mind, the war had been far away in other countries. After the war it seemed as if wars would stay far from us. But after the Russians set off their bomb, it seemed likely they would bomb the United States. I thought the Russians might even bomb Toledo. It was the only big city I knew anything about, so it was the most important city in the world to me. It wasn't far away, and I thought our house might be flattened if the Russians dropped an A-bomb on Toledo.

I was nine years old in 1949, old enough to worry about wars and bombs besides the tornadoes and other scary things that happened around the country. When I went upstairs to bed with my brothers every night, I stayed awake after they went to sleep. I listened to the sound of the airplanes that came over our house on their way to the Toledo airport. They came in low for their approach to the airport, and their piston engines were so loud I could feel the sound against my chest. I knew most of them were "our" planes. They were friendly. I listened for anything strange. Anything new or strange could be the sign of a Russian plane coming to bomb Toledo.

I listened as each plane went over the house and headed for Toledo and prayed that it was not a Russian plane. Still, I waited for the explosion. When there was no explosion and no more planes were on their way, my work was finished for another night, and I went to sleep.

(*Before the Russians came to my boyish attention, probably in about 1946, I noticed that my father's black lunch box had a five-point star stamped into the metal on each end. The star was marked only by its stamped shape; I thought it should be more visible. "Could I paint the stars on your lunch box red?" I asked in total ignorance. "No, I don't think that would be a good idea," my dad replied without explaining. I don't know when I learned why the red star would have been a bad idea at the oil refinery. I didn't know much about communism when I was six.)*

Part Eleven

School Stories

The Harris-Elmore School

The historic heart of Leatherport was once on the riverbank at the south end of Graytown Road, and its educational center was at the Leatherport School just north on Graytown Road. But by 1925, the center of business life and book learning had moved west from Leatherport to Elmore. Harris-Elmore School opened in 1925, and several nearby one-room schools closed. The new school in Elmore was "one giant leap for mankind" in Harris Township.

There were thirty-six kids in my class when we entered first grade in 1945, and there were forty-two in our graduating class in 1957. Those numbers don't mean that we simply gained six kids during our twelve years in school. Over the course of those twelve years, eighty-six different kids were in our class for varying lengths of time, but nineteen of us were together for all twelve years. We were like brothers and sisters, with some of the same affections and annoyances as siblings.

The Harris-Elmore School was made up of "town kids" and "farm kids." My siblings and I counted as farm kids because we lived in the country, even though we didn't have a farm. Like most country kids, we were less wise about town and city life than the kids who lived in town.

The family names in the class lists suggest that Northern European background was the most common, and some names suggest families that may have come from the British Isles. One or two names may be French or Italian. Three Hispanic names are on the list as well.

There were only four hundred kids in the twelve grades back then, so the school was small and bare-bones compared to huge, modern, industrial-scale public schools now. But the Elmore School was devoted to academic quality, and its principal and teachers made sure it happened.

Elmore's Teachers

Teachers at Elmore might be horrified to see me writing about them at all, let alone in a book. After all, I graduated near the bottom of my class and brought little joy to most of them. But they can take pride in the fact that they were at least partly successful with me because I learned to type and have so far stayed out of jail.

If any of my teachers are aware of me writing about them here, they may want to ask God if there is any justice in His world. In any case, it has fallen to me to be the one to tell what I remember of the teachers who tried to civilize and educate me and my classmates between 1945 and 1957.

Because kids in Elmore and the surrounding rural areas attended that one school, it was an important feature of the town and the outlying farms. Our teachers were celebrities of sorts, though we didn't think of them that way when we were kids. They were celebrities because they were known throughout the community, better known than the pastors of the community's several churches. They were expected to be, and generally were, models of good behavior with intellect that commanded respect.

Teachers are subject to the close-up scrutiny of their students, day in and day out, year after year. Sometimes school kids notice unexpected details in their teachers. At least some of their students, like me, tend to remember dramatic incidents more than the teachers' faithfully taught subject matter.

Mr. Lamar Hetrick, Principal and Superintendent

When the Class of 1957 entered Harris-Elmore School in September 1945, the school was led and managed by Mr. Lamar Hetrick. He had come to Elmore from Fremont as an industrial arts teacher in 1940. The superintendent who hired him, Charles R. Housley, had registered for the draft on Valentine's Day 1942 at age forty, just two months after Pearl Harbor. Mr. Hetrick was "drafted" to take over the school, and he became superintendent in 1943.

Lamar Hetrick, humble hometown hero.

He held that position for twenty-five years until Elmore and nearby Woodville were merged into a single school district in 1968. He continued as assistant superintendent until he retired in 1973. Mr. Hetrick became a civic leader and local hero. Besides overseeing the school, he was active in the Grace Lutheran Church, and he taught Sunday school for many years. He was an active leader in the Boy Scouts, the Kiwanis Club, and in the Masonic Lodge.

When my class, the Class of 1957, arrived in 1945, Mr. Hetrick was still early in his career but fully in charge of the school. An aura of authority and dignity surrounded him. Even now I tremble to say his first name, Lamar, since kids back then didn't ever say the first names of teachers, let alone the first name of the school superintendent.

A picture in the online archives of the Elmore Public Library shows the 1944–45 faculty members with Mr. Hetrick by their side. Little did they know that the Class of 1957 would arrive the next year and impact the school in ways they could never have imagined.

(As a sometimes unruly student, I had only a grudging respect for Mr. Hetrick while I was in school. Many years later, after I had become a private school headmaster, I saw him at a Bob Evans Restaurant in Toledo. Mr. Hetrick was up in years by then, but he remembered me and greeted me with a broad smile. We had a friendly conversation, and he bragged about the Kardatzke kids, including my many cousins. It was fortunate that he evidently did not remember my past, or maybe he was just that forgiving. Mr. Hetrick was born in Fremont in 1910 and died in Elmore in 1994.)

Miss Grace Myers – First Grade

Miss Grace Myers was our teacher when the Class of '57 entered first grade in September 1945. The atomic bombs had just dropped on Japan, and the war had ended just in time for us to start school. My older brother Merl must have taken me to my classroom because I was in the right room when the bell rang. I couldn't have made it there without him.

Miss Myers was a kind but stern teacher. She had to be stern to keep order in a classroom of thirty-six kids ranging from five to eight years old. I was one of the five-year-old boys and among the youngest due to my October birthday. I came from a large family, but I had never been with that many kids in one place, even in church.

We kids had assigned seats in desks that were screwed to long, wooden rails so groups of desks could be slid aside for floor cleaning. Each desk had a flip-up seat attached to the desk behind it. Under each desktop there was a shelf for books, papers, pencils, and any personal stuff such as gum or candy secretly smuggled into the school. Each desktop had a large hole for an inkwell, and in our early years we actually used inkwells.

The inkwells held small bottles of ink with screw-on caps and little reservoirs of ink inside. We could fill our fountain pens (pens with a tiny rubber ink reservoir) or dip the point of a simple stylus pen into the ink.

Because inkwells were messy and the ink was easily splattered, most of our schoolwork was done in pencil, the tidier friend of janitors.

To start class that first day, Miss Myers clapped her hands and said in a penetrating, nasal voice, "Little people! Little people!"

We kids were already smart enough to know we were little and to be quiet when the only adult in the room clapped her hands and spoke loudly to us. And we realized immediately that we must be the "little people."

The first educational experience in Miss Myers' classroom was learning to write our first names. We were given big, black beginner's pencils that had thick lead and were at least twice as big around as a regular yellow pencil. Along with the pencils we were given rough, lined paper. I was lucky to have a short name: Nyle. Learning to print our names was harder for Lowell, Shirley, and Beatrice.

Although it wasn't an educational experience, we had birthday parties in first grade, or at least there was one party that I remember. One of the girls brought cupcakes for the whole class, and we tried to sing Happy Birthday to her. The party made an indelible impression on my unsophisticated mind. It may have been an exception to a school rule, because no other birthday parties have lodged in my memory bank.

An especially exciting moment came in the fall of 1945 when one of the country girls, Faye Rothert, waved a banana in the air and yelled, "Surprise!" It was a big surprise to see a banana at school, and we all clapped. Bananas were a rarity during the war because there had been little civilian shipping. Shipping from banana-growing areas in Central America had been disrupted by the threat of enemy submarines. Later in first grade, when bananas became more commonly available, our classroom at lunchtime smelled of peanut butter and bananas every day.

After lunch at our desks in the classroom, Miss Myers read stories to us. Some of the kids may have fallen asleep, but I was sitting near the front and was lost in the stories. There was an especially enchanting series of stories about a boy living in a stockade in a jungle, maybe in India. There were scary tigers in the jungle, and the stockade protected the boy and his family. A drawbridge over a moat and a huge door protected kids inside from tigers and other dangers. Those stories led all of us first graders to believe that there could be fun in reading when we grew older, but reading was hard work for us in first grade. We started reading "Dick and Jane" books, and all of us can still read "Look and see Jane" if we really need to.

Sometime during first grade, a new boy named Douglas Pickard came into our class. We called him Doug. He sat on the other side of the room from me, over by the windows, so I never talked with him in first grade. Because of Doug, we all learned something useful.

One day Miss Myers gave each of us a sheet of paper with a picture printed in bold, black ink. She gave us another piece of plain white paper and told us to put it on top of the picture. When we smoothed the top sheet, we could see the printed form underneath. Miss Myers told us to trace the design onto the top paper, so we all began struggling to do what she had said.

Suddenly Miss Myers said quite loudly, "Now you sit down! What are you doing there?"

I looked around the room and saw the new boy, Doug, standing at the window next to his desk with his papers pressed against the window.

"It's easier to see through the paper this way," he said. It must have been true because he had already done more than I had.

"That doesn't matter," Miss Myers said. "Now take your seat."

Doug Pickard sat down and worked at his tracing at his desk like the rest of us. I thought to myself, *That was a good idea. That kid must really be smart.*

(Doug Pickard became an aeronautical engineer and was on a team that designed one of the early moon rockets.

Before entering first grade my tonsils were surgically removed. It was a common procedure before kids started school and was supposed to prevent infections that might lodge in the tonsils. A doctor held an ether-soaked cloth over my nose and mouth while nurses held me down until the sweet-smelling ether put me into a deep sleep. I dreamed I was winning a footrace against a streamlined train engine, showing I was "advanced for my age." I was ready for the rigors of school life.)

Mrs. Mildred Arnold – Second Grade

On the first day of second grade, my seat was on the front row. The teacher stood right in front of me when she first spoke to the class, and she was very tall, much taller than Miss Myers. Her name was *Mrs.* Arnold. I had been in school only a year, but I already knew that "Mrs." meant she was married.

Only a couple of memories have survived from second grade. The first was learning to write my last name, "Kardatzke." Just seeing it here in this book shows that I was not as lucky as I had been in first grade when I only had to write my first name, "Nyle."

To begin this learning experience, Mrs. Arnold printed our first and last names on the top line of our lined papers and told us to fill the page, copying and recopying what she had printed for us. When she gave me my paper, I just stared at it on my desk. When I didn't begin immediately, Mrs. Arnold came to my desk.

"That's your first and last name," she explained. "That big word is 'Kardatzke.'"

I had heard that word before, but I only knew it had something to do with my Gramma and Grampa. The letters looked like a lot of sharp objects that had crashed together. I wondered if I would ever learn how to print that huge name. Fortunately, due to the perseverance of my teachers, by sixth grade or maybe sooner, I could not only print my full name, I could write my first and last names in cursive script.

In second grade, I persuaded my mother to have a birthday party at our house for me and a few kids from my class. That party was for my seventh birthday, and my mother held it on our front porch. I only remember inviting three girls from the class, probably because I was vaguely in love with each of them. We sat in a circle on the porch for cake and Kool-Aid. My mother may have made party favors for us. I remember that she made sailor caps from yellow crepe paper. I wondered if they were the right kind, since I had never attended a birthday party. Fortunately, no one else remembers the party.

The other big event in second grade was the basket factory fire. It happened on a sunny, hot fall day. It may have been about lunchtime when we heard the town siren blow, calling the volunteer firemen to come from their jobs in town and on farms.

The basket factory was one of Elmore's main industries. There, thin strips of wood were bent and stapled into fruit baskets, from small quart-size baskets for strawberries to full bushel baskets for apples or pears or tomatoes or sweet corn.

As soon as he heard the siren, one of the town kids pointed out the window. "Look! Smoke!" he said in a loud stage whisper.

Clouds of brown and black smoke were blowing past the school, just beyond the street in front of our classroom. It was like war pictures. We all jumped up and ran to the windows. After we had a good look at the clouds of smoke, we went back to whatever we were doing. Mrs. Arnold closed the windows to keep the smoke out, even though it was a hot day, and the basket factory burned to the ground.

Miss Mattie Heckman – Third Grade

Mattie Heckman lived in a log cabin and
helped the author recover from pneumonia.

Our vast learning in second grade prepared us for third grade with Miss Heckman. She had gray hair tied up in a bun, and she seemed like a kind, old grandmother. But she wasn't a grandmother at all because she was "Miss" and had no children. Miss Heckman became my favorite grade school teacher.

I nearly died in third grade. Maybe I didn't nearly die, but I did have pneumonia and was in the Fremont Memorial Hospital for a week. I might not have survived had it not been for a new medicine called penicillin.

My recovery at home was slow, so I was out of school for a month and fell behind in my schoolwork. When I went back to school, Miss Mattie Heckman was glad to see me. She welcomed me back and was especially nice to me. She explained things to me that I had missed, and she made up special homework assignments for me that I could do in spite of missing the classwork.

When I had been back in school a few weeks, my mother heard on the radio that kids could write letters to the radio station about "My Favorite Teacher." Mama asked if I would like to write about Miss Heckman.

Mama's question reminded me of my love for Miss Heckman and how she had helped me after I had been so sick. "She *is* my favorite teacher!" I said, and I sat down to write. I don't know what I wrote, but it felt good to be writing about Miss Heckman. I probably wrote only two or three sentences, and that was hard work at the time. Mama mailed my letter to the radio station.

A few weeks later, Mama said, "You have some mail! It's about the letter you wrote about Miss Heckman!"

Mama held out a fancy-looking paper with designs around the edge. It looked important, maybe like something from Bible times or from a king.

"It's a certificate about your letter. It says you wrote a good letter about Miss Heckman. Look, here's her name, and down here is your name."

I looked at the certificate and could see the two names. Printed in large letters at the top of the certificate was "My Favorite Teacher." Underneath those words was "Mattie Heckman." Other printing filled the rest of the certificate, and my name was there near the bottom.

Leatherport, Ohio

"Miss Heckman can hang this certificate on the wall or put it in her scrapbook," Mama explained. "We need to take this to her at school as soon as we can."

Three days later, Mama came to the school after all the other kids had gone home and I met her outside. Miss Heckman was at her desk getting ready for the next day. We went in, and Mama nudged me to take the certificate to Miss Heckman. I watched as she read it and then read it again. At first she didn't look up at me. When she did look up, there were tears in her eyes. Then she looked at me with her wise smile, the kind of smile that mainly comes to old, kind people.

"Thank you," Miss Heckman said. And I knew she meant it.

(The city of Fremont had not only a hospital but also a radio station. At about noon each day, WFRO had a program called "The Hospital Report," and my mother listened to it often. I paid little attention because it was mostly about older people I didn't know or who had diseases I had never heard of. WFRO also reported on people admitted to or released from the Magruder Hospital in Port Clinton. The information and entertainment in those programs ended in 1996 when a new law was passed regarding patient confidentiality.

Miss Heckman was born in 1893 in the log cabin where she lived until her passing in 1976. She taught twelve years in rural schools and then thirty-nine years in the Harris-Elmore School. Yellow siding covered the logs on the sides of her house during my school years. Mildred Magsig donated the home to the Elmore Historical Society in 1981. The siding was removed, and the logs underneath were revealed. When Mattie Heckman's log house was moved to Elmore, my older brother was there to witness the event. A flatbed truck was to receive the ancient cabin, and a farmer brought a large tractor with a hydraulic forklift in front. The farmer gently slid the tractor's prongs under the cabin and tried to slowly lift Mattie Heckman's cabin onto the truck. The strain was too much, and down came the logs, plaster, roof, and all in a heap. Historical Society volunteers and onlookers gathered all the pieces and hauled them into Elmore for reassembly. The reassembled and restored cabin is open to visitors on a regular schedule.)

Mrs. Mabel Rozine – Fourth Grade

Mrs. Rozine had snow-white hair, and her family roots stretched back to the American Revolution. To us fourth graders, she seemed old enough to have been in the American Revolution. By fourth grade, I had become a restive, smart-mouth kid who loved to stir things up with funny remarks. I was sometimes the only one who thought my remarks were funny, so I had to laugh at my own comments.

For reasons I can't recall, I was often at odds with Mrs. Rozine. It may have had something to do with my smart mouth and the fact that I didn't do my schoolwork very well. My most distinct memory of her, however, is from November 11, 1948. The date remains in my memory because it was Armistice Day, in memory of the day when World War I had ended in 1918, exactly thirty years earlier.

At 11:00 a.m., the town siren sounded from the top of the Elmore water tower and church bells rang. Mrs. Rozine stopped whatever we were doing.

"Be quiet, children," she directed, and we actually were quiet to hear the siren wailing.

"This is Armistice Day," she said. "It's the day World War I ended."

We had heard of World War I, but we knew next to nothing about it. We only knew that old soldiers from World War I always led the Memorial Day parade in town.

Mrs. Rozine explained that Armistice Day was the day when World War I had ended, and it ended on the eleventh hour of the eleventh day of the eleventh month in 1918. The way she said it made it easy to remember: 11-11-11. As she talked, her speech became more emotional, almost angry.

"We shouldn't keep celebrating Armistice Day!" she declared. "World War I was supposed to be 'the war to end all wars.' But it didn't work. We just had another war! We should stop celebrating Armistice Day!"

What she's saying makes sense, I thought, *but what about all those old men who fought in World War I? We shouldn't forget about them.*

I must have had the mind of a statesman that day because November 11 was renamed Veteran's Day in 1954 to honor all veterans of all the wars.

The new name seemed to me to be a signal that we might have more wars in the future, and we would need a way to honor all those who would serve in all those future wars. I was right.

Mrs. Rozine had already told us more than once that her husband had fought in World War I. During one telling she said, "My husband smokes, but he fought in World War I, so I think he earned the right to smoke."

I didn't question her logic. I just wondered if something would happen in the future that would be serious enough to give me permission to smoke, something I had longed to do since 1945 when I'd seen so many former soldiers smoking.

Mrs. Garnet Weber – Fifth Grade

On the day our class entered fifth grade in 1949, the world was at peace, even though the Russians had set off an A-bomb on August 29, right before school started. Our teacher that year was Mrs. Garnet Weber.

Like all the teachers, Mrs. Weber dressed professionally, but she seemed even more professional than most of the female teachers because she often wore women's business suits. She had dark hair, nearly black, and she was slim. Her dark suits accented her dark hair, and her close-fitting skirts were the standard, fairly long postwar length. Her school photo shows that she was an attractive woman, but her beauty was lost on us fifth-grade kids.

About this time, I read in My Weekly Reader that the world would run out of oil in twenty years. This was sad news, because I was looking forward to driving a car, and I might have only fifteen years to drive before the world ran out of oil.

Mrs. Weber's professional manner brought order to the classroom spontaneously most of the time. There was dignity about her that even fifth graders didn't want to violate with bad behavior. Her personal life was a mystery to us, except we knew she was Catholic, and her husband was a dentist.

Fifth grade must have gone smoothly because I remember so little about it. My grades were good enough to allow me to pass into sixth grade the following year, but no one would have accused me of being a good student. School was a struggle for me and sometimes for my teachers.

Mrs. Helen Mercer – Sixth Grade

Sixth grade was my most immemorial year in the Elmore School, but I wasn't the only troublemaker. Even some of the well-behaved students participated in our class' rebellion against Mrs. Mercer. If there were any innocent members of our class, I can't name them now. I was not among the innocent.

The trouble we inflicted on Mrs. Mercer must have contributed to the end of her teaching career. She left after that year, and her picture from the 1944-45 school year suggests she may have been the oldest teacher in the school, even seven years before our class descended upon her in 1950.

To her credit, Mrs. Mercer endowed us with an artistic skill that some of us probably can still perform. She taught us how to fold strips of paper into Christmas stars. We folded the strips in a certain way to make a 3-D modified Star of David with two points at the top, at the bottom, and on each side. Four conical points jutted out on the front and back of each star. After we shaped them, we dipped them into melted paraffin and sprinkled them with metallic glitter. The stars are my brightest memory of our sixth-grade year.

Mr. Richard Eldridge – Seventh-Grade Homeroom

My classmates and I entered the junior high school in seventh grade. This change meant that we moved from room to room during the school day and had a different teacher for each subject instead of getting all our book learning from one teacher all day. Being in junior high was said to be preparing us for the maturity we would need in senior high school.

Our homeroom teacher, Mr. Eldridge, was good-natured, well-dressed, and good-looking for such an old man—though he may have been only thirty years old. In addition to being our homeroom teacher, he taught history, and he introduced us to the Holy Roman Empire. He said several times that the Holy Roman Empire was neither holy nor Roman nor an empire. I have valued that knowledge all my life.

I don't remember being in big trouble that year. I played an alto horn in the band that year, but I had little idea of how the alto line should sound, even with the notes in front of me. It was the last time I tried to play a band instrument, and the musical world has been better for that.

Mrs. Dora Coleman – Eighth-Grade Homeroom

Mrs. Coleman was my eighth-grade English teacher. She had white hair and a dignified manner. She valued history and patriotism like Mrs. Rozine, my fourth-grade teacher, and the two of them resembled each other in appearance and temperament. There was a degree of formality about Mrs. Coleman that seemed to raise the level of civilization in her classroom. We were on the brink of high school, and Mrs. Coleman did her best to prepare us for that big step.

That year Bill Kuhlman's parents sponsored a Christmas party for our class at their farmhouse out in the country. Mrs. Coleman was brave to risk her professional reputation by having an event outside the school building, and it was equally courageous of the Kuhlman family to have the party in their home. It was a large, white frame house, and it was as elegant as any house I had ever seen. There were snacks and party games. During one of the games, I fell in love with one of the girls in the class. It was a one-night romance that didn't go beyond my looking deeply into her brown eyes, but that was a dizzying experience. I couldn't have handled anything more intimate.

Mrs. Coleman directed us in a play during our eighth-grade year. My character was an eccentric, somewhat scientific older man in odd clothing. The casting seemed to say a lot about me that year, and it was the type of oddball character I played throughout my high school years.

Sometime later that year Mrs. Coleman introduced us to the "minuet," a formal, stylized dance from the time of the American Revolution. The gym was the only place large enough for this special activity, and it called for social skills beyond most of us eighth-graders. We boys had to actually look directly at girls and hold hands with them or lock elbows with them as we did a little skipping, hopping, bowing dance. The motions of the dance were awkward enough, but the dance itself presented a moral and spiritual dilemma for me. My church was against dancing, and I didn't know of an exception for a historical dance like we were doing. I risked my immortal soul on the minuet that day, but I later adopted a theology that allowed enough divine forgiveness to cover even the minuet.

Shortly before spring break (which we called Easter vacation), our class went on a field trip to the Elmore water plant. Field trips were not common, so our walk to the water treatment plant was a big deal. The added drama in the trip was the fact that the water plant was next to the water tower, the tallest structure in Elmore. My contribution to the day was rolling on my side down the grassy incline that surrounded the water treatment pond. It was not my finest hour.

Mrs. Coleman decided our class would plant a maple tree on Arbor Day, and luckily the weather was good. We marched all the way from the school to a small park on the bank of the Portage River. We held a short ceremony in what is now Harry Witte Memorial Park, and one of the students read "Trees" by Mr. Joyce Kilmer, a writer who died in 1918 in France during World War I. We evidently planted the tree well because it was still standing there in 2020.

The most amazing thing about my eighth-grade year was that Mrs. Coleman chose me, of all people, to recite the poem "Flanders Fields" at the patriotic ceremony following the town parade on Memorial Day. It was the biggest, most terrifying public performance of my life up to that time. Mrs. Coleman gave me a copy of the poem and told me to memorize it. I practiced at home and recited the poem to my mother and then at school for Mrs. Coleman. I had the poem down pat by Memorial Day.

Leatherport, Ohio

Before the parade and the crowd arrived, Mrs. Coleman showed me where to stand to recite the poem. Soon the band and the rest of the crowd came. I hadn't realized until then how large the crowd would be. It was the largest crowd I had ever seen. The whole town of Elmore gathered around the small plaza. I didn't know until then that there would be a microphone and an electric loudspeaker to amplify the speakers' voices, including mine.

The first speaker may have been the mayor. I was too young and too scared to know who he was. The sound system crackled a little, and he began to speak. His voice boomed out over the crowd and across the Portage River and echoed back to us. The sound of his voice made him sound ten feet tall, but he was just the normal size for a mayor.

Soon it was time for my part. The person leading the program said, "Now we will hear the World War I poem, 'Flanders Fields,' recited by Nyle Kardatzke from the eighth grade."

He looked at me. Mrs. Coleman gave me a slight nudge. I stepped to the microphone. I clasped my hands behind my back and announced the poem.

"'Flanders Fields,' by Colonel John MacCrae," I chirped in my high-pitched eighth-grade voice.

I had never spoken through an amplifier, and it made my voice sound childish and very, very loud. My voice chirped and echoed across the river. My knees began shaking, but there was nothing to do but plunge ahead. My memorization didn't fail me, and I marched out the words of the poem in spite of the sound of my voice:

> *In Flanders fields the poppies blow*
> *Between the crosses, row on row,*
> *That mark our place; and in the sky*
> *The larks, still bravely singing, fly*
> *Scarce heard amid the guns below.*
>
> *We are the dead. Short days ago*
> *We lived, felt dawn, saw sunset glow,*
> *Loved, and were loved, and now we lie*
> *In Flanders fields.*

Take up our quarrel with the foe:
To you from failing hands we throw
The torch; be yours to hold it high.
If ye break faith with us who die
We shall not sleep, though poppies grow
In Flanders fields.

My knees were still shaking when I finished, and the last echoes of my thin little voice faded away across the river. I was glad my knees didn't buckle when I stepped away from the microphone. The crowd applauded politely, the program continued majestically, and the day ended when a small group of veterans fired their rifles over the river.

The crowd dispersed and the street was quiet again, almost as quiet as on Flanders fields. Eighth grade was over. I had given my first public speech, and it had been in front of the whole town. I was ready for high school.

Mr. Clarence Egert – Ninth-Grade Homeroom and Math

Entering high school in 1953 was a big deal. My classmates and I were warming up for our take-off out of school and into the big world. Ninth grade was the beginning of the real thing. Seventh and eighth grades had prepared us, and we were proud to have arrived. We were included among the oldest, boldest, strongest, tallest, smartest, best-looking, and coolest kids in school. It was heady stuff.

Adding to the excitement of being in high school was the arrival of seven new students from Benton Township, just to the north of Harris Township. The kids had attended elementary school in Benton Township, but for high school they had to choose between Elmore and Oak Harbor, the first town east of Elmore. Four girls and three boys joined our class, and they enriched the genetic mix. We became a stronger, more sophisticated race of ninth-graders than we could have been without them.

Mr. Egert was our homeroom teacher, and we met in his math classroom. He was younger than most of our earlier teachers, and he was handsome. He had dark, curly hair, and he dressed well. He was confident, and he seemed competent. He was our math teacher as well as homeroom teacher, and he introduced us to the mysteries of algebra. We learned to use letters of the alphabet to represent numbers, and we learned to understand formulas in equations. We became far more sophisticated intellectually than when we merely used numbers to add, subtract, multiply, and divide.

Very little was out of place in Mr. Egert's math class, and it had a relaxed, business-like feel. Only one moment of unintended humor survives in my mind. Mr. Egert was explaining positive and negative numbers. He stood before the class and motioned downward to show where negative numbers reside. He then motioned upward to show the power and glory of positive numbers. But in showing the upward power of positive numbers, Mr. Egert pointed upward with his middle finger. Our jaws dropped.

We had learned the rude power of the middle finger sometime in grade school, so we couldn't believe we were seeing it right in algebra class. No one said anything. I don't think anyone dared to laugh. We waited for the embarrassing moment to pass, and we set it aside as an endearing, memorable moment with a much-appreciated teacher.

Mr. Ray Goetschius – Tenth-Grade Homeroom and Social Studies

Mr. Ray Goetschius must have been my homeroom teacher in my sophomore year. I remember him better as our social studies teacher. He had an amiable personality, but he projected an aura of authority like a soldier.

We learned that he was not only a veteran of World War II but also had been a prisoner of war. During his tour of duty, he was captured by the enemy and spent a long time in a German prison camp. He may have been a prisoner for over a year. We saw a special strength in him that must have been grown during that time.

I remember Mr. Goetschius as soft-spoken, so it must have been his military past that burst out one afternoon when the school buses were loading. He charged onto my half-full school bus because he had seen a boy spitting and throwing trash on passing students who were boarding another bus. He grabbed the offender, shook him, and delivered a forceful sermon. I was thankful I was not the guilty boy.

Mrs. Catherine Anstead – Eleventh-Grade Homeroom and English in the Year I Didn't Drop out of School

Through no fault of hers, I have few memories of Catherine Anstead from my junior year in high school. She was a low-key, dignified teacher, and I never doubted her competence. She taught English and Latin.

One memory of her stands out. It was an incident that convinced me I was attending a high-quality school. I was babbling in class, speaking out of turn while she was leading the class in a discussion. Maybe I was fumbling to answer a question, and I must have been going on and on. Mrs. Anstead broke in to my babbling.

"Nyle is giving a soliloquy," she said. "We'll continue with class when he's finished."

The dignity of her rebuke stopped me. I stopped my soliloquy, struck down by the power of the English language. I don't know why, but I somehow had a vague idea of the meaning of *"soliloquy."* I was embarrassed to have my chattering elevated to the level of literature. Over the years, I grew to appreciate the fact that I attended a school where a teacher could take me to task so eloquently.

My junior year in high school marked a turning point. I don't know how long I had whined and complained at home about school, but my complaining had so exasperated my dad that he went to Mr. Hetrick's house on a Saturday and picked up papers to sign so I could drop out of school.

My dad showed me the papers and said I could drop out of school any time, get a job, and seek my fortune. I had turned sixteen in October, the age at which a kid could drop out of school in Ohio. I already had a driver's license, so I could drive to work if I left school. If he didn't sign the papers and let me drop out of school, my dad said, he didn't want to hear any more complaining about it.

That shut me up. He shocked me into realizing that I didn't *really* want to drop out of school. I began to train myself not to complain, at least not so much, and not around home. I decided to begin learning a few study habits. Mrs. Anstead had delivered an elegant, intellectual rebuke. My dad had quietly brought up the heavy ammunition of the real world.

Mrs. Alvina Kontak – Twelfth-Grade Homeroom and English

During my junior year, when it occurred to me that I should probably start taking school seriously, I had no idea where school might be leading. In my senior year, Mrs. Kontak made it seem worthwhile.

Mrs. Kontak taught the Senior English Composition course, and she had the stature and style of a college teacher. She gave us the feeling that we were indeed at the top of our high school world and that we were approaching graduation. I realized the next year that her class had been like freshman English composition class when I accidentally went to college.

I have always prized one crowning moment in Mrs. Kontak's class that gave me an inkling that I might be college material. We were asked to write a descriptive paragraph about something we liked to remember. I wrote about a mountain stream I had seen on a family trip to Colorado where clear, cold water flowed over beautiful, round rocks and trout frolicked in the ripples near the edge. The paragraph was short, but it was well-written.

When we read our paragraphs to the class, Mrs. Kontak heaped praise on what I had written. "That was beautiful, Nyle!" she exclaimed. "I didn't know you could write so clearly and beautifully!"

I blushed with pride and satisfaction. It was one of the proudest moments of my high school career.

Mrs. Phyllis Barker – Typing

Several other high school subject matter teachers stand out in my memory besides the homeroom teachers. I have already bragged that I can type. I owe that skill to Mrs. Barker. She saved my academic life.

Although Mrs. Kontak had encouraged me in writing, typing class in my senior year was the major achievement of my twelve years in the Harris-Elmore School. At least it seemed so to me at the time. If I hadn't learned to type, writing term papers longhand in college would have been slow, painful work for me and gruesome experiences for my professors. My handwriting would have betrayed me for the semi-illiterate boy I was.

The typing classroom was just off the second-floor hallway overlooking the older students' playground. It was divided from the business classroom by a row of windows. I sat next to Beatrice Hetrick on the hallway side of the room, and I bantered with the poor girl all year. She was shy, and I think her tolerant giggling made me bolder in my bantering.

The typewriters were big, office-style machines that made a satisfying clatter, especially when we built up some speed. The gratifying noise of slamming the carriage back to the right at the end of a sentence on those old manual typewriters was its own reward.

By performing a series of typing drills that started very simply and became more complex, we learned what was called "touch typing." It was amazing that our fingers could remember the locations of all those keys, and we had to look down only once in a while to find a key.

We somehow measured our typing speed, but I'm not sure how. Mrs. Barker must have used a watch to measure a minute and had us type from a specific document. Some of the girls had the highest speeds, naturally. I was pleased to be clocked once at 42 words per minute. There may have been a faint smell of burning oil when I stopped.

287

Leatherport, Ohio

Mr. Burl Barker – Vocational Agriculture

"Vocational Agriculture" is a course title that must have been made up to dignify the class and make it sound a step or two higher than "Farming." While farming was at the heart of vocational agriculture, there was a scientific and academic aspect to it that might surprise people who weren't there. I wandered into Mr. Barker's Vocational Agriculture course in ninth grade out of a misperception. I thought I might actually become a farmer as my vocation, and not just because "vocation" was in the name of the course.

When I was in eighth grade, Mr. Hetrick was supervising our high school registration. Only three courses of study were available in our high school: agriculture, industrial arts, and the college prep track. I thought I knew what two of them would be like, but I was curious about the college prep track. I saw that it started with a Latin class.

"What do you do in Latin class?" I asked in total ignorance.

"You conjugate verbs!" Mr. Hetrick fairly barked on that hectic day.

Conjugate verbs! I knew vaguely what that meant after years of doubting the value of grammar in English classes. I had heard the term and wanted no more of it. I signed up for agriculture, assuming I wouldn't have to conjugate verbs there or perhaps ever again.

It would be unfair for me to share all my vast learning in "Vo-Ag" and make you feel obligated to read about it. A few highlights may be enough to suggest why choosing "Vo-Ag" was one of the more productive blunders of my academic career.

Two major projects outside school were required of every future farmer in the Vocational Agriculture. These were not academic, bookwork projects. They were physical projects, and they involved living things, both plants and animals. To top off the learning experience, students were to earn or lose money by doing them. I chose to raise pigs and care for our family's orchard. The projects were combined: I raised pigs in our orchard and raised apples and pears there, too.

My pig project involved three mother pigs, called sows, of three different breeds: Hampshire, Yorkshire, and Spotted Poland China. The three sows had different success records in farrowing piglets. I never had more than two sows at a time. Over the three years I raised pigs, I must have worked with a total population of twenty-five to thirty pigs. Some of the pigs had short lives. Some large litters of Hampshires and Yorkshires survived to go to market, but nearly all the Poland China piglets died of milk fever one grim, cold winter. I lost a lot of my dad's money on pigs while I was a future farmer.

Pigs and the merry-go-round in our yard. Bertha, my first sow, having breakfast. The truck-axle merry-go-round is in the center. The old Gleckler/Sandrock house is in the distance.

As part of his role in my project, Mr. Barker came to my house to perform "surgery" on the little boy piglets from each new litter. We rounded them up and took them to the garage in a big cardboard box. He first dabbed them behind an ear with alcohol and slid the sharp edge of a hollow tube under the skin. A plunger inside the tube pushed a tiny antibiotic pill under the skin. The antibiotic was to prevent infection that might come from the next procedure: castrating the boy pigs. Castration was done primarily because it caused them to gain weight faster than if they had grown to become boars, the big daddies of the pig world. It also eliminated the chance of any piggish hanky-panky or unwanted pregnancies in the pig lots.

For the castration operation, I had to hold a little pig on its back on my lap and grip its hind legs upward with its bottom pointed toward Mr. Barker. He disinfected the area with alcohol, made a quick slit, popped out a testicle, and severed the connecting tube with a rubbing motion of the knife that reduced bleeding. The second testicle was popped out, and soon the neutered little pig was back in the box.

One after another, I selected boy pigs and held them while Mr. Barker performed the surgery until all the boys had lost their piggish boy-ness. The girl pigs suffered no such indignity, but theirs was not an easy life. Eventually the girls, like the boys, would end up in Tank's Meats slaughterhouse in town.

My pigs humiliated me as a farmer-to-be one day by rooting their noses under the fence and getting out into the yard just when I arrived home on the school bus. I was a junior, and that day I had finally been brave enough to sit with the eighth-grade girl I was in love with. The pigs in the yard probably gave her a horrifying vision of what life would be like with me. We never married. We never even went on a date.

Tending the orchard was my other project. I learned the rules for pruning apple, pear, peach, apricot, and cherry trees. Spraying for bugs and fungi was essential, and I borrowed a gasoline-powered sprayer from a neighbor. I covered the trees with mercury and arsenic sprays, and I'm grateful I haven't yet come down with a weird disorder from those chemicals (even though some might say I just don't recognize the disorders those toxins have given me).

In the Vo-Ag shop, we learned skills denied most high school kids. For example, we learned gas and electric welding, and I built the steel frame for a trailer that my dad used for decades. I even honed my welding skills in a night class at a public high school in Toledo. We learned blacksmith skills on a forge in our shop with a hand-crank blower. It created a flame hot enough to turn metal rods white-hot for hammering into chisels or bending into the needed shapes. I sometimes thought of the words from the poem "The Village Blacksmith" by Henry Wadsworth Longfellow while hammering hot chisels: "Under a spreading chestnut tree, the village smithy stands . . ." We also learned about fertilizers, crop rotation, soil conservation, contour plowing, diseases of plants and animals, land judging, cattle judging, and farm bookkeeping.

Insolent Hampshire pigs, formerly boys, who tunneled under the fence.

We future farmers took field trips as well, including one to a breeding farm where we saw a gigantic bull amorously jump on a cow. The culmination was interrupted when a farm worker slipped a hard rubber sleeve over the bull's organ at just the right moment to capture the sperm-bearing semen. It was a demonstration unlikely to be on the curriculum in a city school.

Mr. Barker also led us in some money-making projects that included scrap drives for metal and paper. We went to farms and collected large and small metal objects to sell to a scrapyard. In other years, we had scrap paper drives and we sold cider in the fall. We raised enough money for our annual out-of-town field trips. We took train trips to St. Louis, Chicago, and Washington, DC, with Mr. Barker as our heroic chaperone.

Most surprising to city folk is the fact that in Vo-Ag we also studied debate, public speaking, and parliamentary procedure. The farmers of America's future were being trained not only for scientific farming but for mature civic responsibilities. Having been party to hundreds of business meetings in my working life, I'm convinced I know more parliamentary procedure than most lawyers because of my agricultural schooling.

The Future Farmers of America organization is still strong and healthy, and it may still live by the FFA Creed I learned in Vo-Ag class. Alas, my farming projects were financial failures. My herd of pigs was caught in the notorious hog cycle when too many farmers raised pigs, and I had to sell them at a loss. As for the orchard, my apples barely paid for the toxins I sprayed on them. I have lived by my wits in cities ever since I left the farm.

Mr. James Smith – Football
Before there was JFK, there was Coach Smith

Coach Jim Smith was the school's own version of John F. Kennedy. He was handsome with a square jaw, athletic build, and an infectious smile. Above all, like Kennedy, he had been on a PT (Patrol Torpedo) boat in the South Pacific during the war. He taught social studies and coached football. In his social studies class, we felt we were part of the war. In the classroom, he was spellbinding. He taught history, and he could tell some hair-raising war stories. If I had known back then that I would be writing about him now, I would have paid more attention and asked more questions, especially about his PT boat.

Because of him, even skinny runts like me were eager to be on the football team. I weighed in at 97 pounds my freshman year, almost like the 98-pound weaklings in the Charles Atlas body-building ads. Another kid weighed in at 92 pounds and saved a shred of my dignity. Before the school year began, we endured early morning practices on hazy, humid summer mornings, yelling as we did jumping jacks to alert the neighbors that we were there. Out on the field, Coach Smith built our confidence and directed us to occasional wins. The most memorable game of the 1953 season was our victory over Genoa, 64-0. Our least memorable game was our 81-0 loss to them the next year.

I may have bulked up to 130 pounds by my junior year, but I could still be run over by a 185-pound fullback. That fullback was my cousin, Lauren Kardatzke. I was playing linebacker one afternoon when he came running at full speed through the gap I was to defend. He was a powerful but kind boy, and since he was my cousin, I was willing to risk my life trying to tackle him. I took three steps toward him with my head lowered. The crash may not have made much noise, but my small, frail body was compressed by the impact. I survived the impact, but it may have been the last time I tried to tackle my cousin head-on. Lauren Kardatzke won a football scholarship at William and Mary. I had no football scholarship anywhere.

My other near-death football experience was on a punt return in practice. My team had punted. The ball was received by Duane Lohr, a tall, handsome, strong boy a year or two ahead of me in school. I was one of the first down the field, and Duane veered toward me. Self-preservation led me to sidestep him as a matador would sidestep an onrushing bull. I swooped down and grabbed for one of his feet. My hand connected with his right foot and I felt a terrific shock. All my joints and ligaments were jerked out of place. The ground shook, and I glanced up to see that I had tripped Duane Lohr in full flight and he had fallen mightily to the turf. It may have been the greatest moment of my athletic career.

My junior year football season was shortened by a knee injury, and I was discouraged by my bench-sitting my senior year. Leaving football at mid-season was one of my wiser high school decisions.

Mr. Charles Rymers — Basketball Coach and Science

Coach Charles Rymers taught freshman biology, and he might have been new to the school during my freshman year. He seemed young, even to us raw thirteen-year-olds in the fall of 1953. He was so young that it was difficult to call him "Mr. Rymers." Behind his back, we called him "Charlie," sometimes affectionately and sometimes not so much.

Charlie Rymers was a product of our very own school, a rare distinction. He lived on one of the oldest farms in the area, just across the river from downtown Elmore. There was even a cemetery next to his farm called the Rymers Cemetery, and his remains are buried there.

My only distinct memory of scientific learning in freshman science was gathering "broadleaf plantains" and other vegetation from the athletic practice fields to start our biology scrapbooks. Had it not been for freshman science, I still would not know the term "broadleaf plantain." I can spot one of those in a plant leaf lineup every time.

Coach Rymers' skills were most evident on the basketball court. He led the Elmore Bulldogs into the state tournament games at least one year and maybe two while I was in school. Elmore didn't make it to the final rounds of the tournament, but the sight of our boys playing in some other school's gym far from Elmore was a thrill. Coach Rymers attributed his coaching success to a brown suit he wore to all the games. He called it his "lucky brown suit." Brown seemed the wrong color for a heroic suit, but it worked for Coach Charlie Rymers.

In my senior year, Coach Rymers reported in science class that some vandals had taken his young son's jack-o'-lantern pumpkin from the front porch and splattered it in his front yard. To some of us, it sounded like an accusation, as though we had done it. To others it seemed like a wrong that should be righted. A posse was assembled that evening, and it converged on Lowell Knieriem's father's farm. He had a field of ripe pumpkins, and the best ones had already been taken to market. The remaining pumpkins needed a special mission at the end of their pumpkin lives. Car trunks were loaded with pumpkins and silently unloaded in Mr. Rymers' front yard that night.

In class the next day, Mr. Rymers reported the miraculous pumpkin crop in his front yard. He said his son was happy. The story might have disappeared from town history had the *Toledo Blade* not heard of it and run the short story, "119 Pumpkins in Teacher's Yard." Look up the story in the Elmore Library archives.

Mr. Herbert Katko – Assistant Football Coach

Mr. Katko was the most ferocious of our high school teachers and coaches. He was an assistant football coach during two of my three years on the football bench. He coached the defensive line at least part of the time.

I learned a lot from Mr. Katko. Just one example should suffice. I was playing guard on offense during practice, and I was supposed to block a linebacker. Mr. Katko had taken the linebacker position to train guards on dealing with linebackers. I headed for him to make my block, and he decked me with such force that my ears were ringing for a few minutes. I learned a lot from that.

Mr. Katko was also the teacher who most actively prosecuted my brother Owen after he dropped a chair from the business classroom window. The chair landed near a teacher, and Mr. Katko went into a fevered investigation. The finger of guilt quickly pointed at Owen, but Owen was a good student with a clean record at school, and he was a juvenile according to Ohio law. He did no prison time.

(A more complete account of the chair incident is included later in this book.)

....

School Janitors

Teachers were not the only adults in the school who influenced us in our educational and emotional maturation. We kids especially loved the janitors. They had no power or authority over us except by virtue of their dignity, their valuable work, and their friendly nature. Their work was straightforward, and we could understand it, unlike some of the mysteries of the teachers' work.

The janitors had a sociable, jolly side. We seldom saw them in their sanctuary in the furnace room unless we were sent there on an errand. A degree of mystery about their role at the school added to our respect for them.

When I was lucky enough to be sent on an errand to the furnace room, I usually found the janitors smoking and telling each other stories. The room was warm enough to make me want to doze off, but the men were always in a lively conversation surrounded by a haze of pipe and cigar smoke. The pleasant scene made me want to become a janitor.

The janitors' most dramatic moments came when someone "threw up" or "heaved" or "barfed" or "tossed their cookies" in class. I was an eyewitness to this drama several times. The drama began when a student suddenly spouted a geyser of partially digested food onto the classroom floor. Another student was then sent to the furnace room to ask a janitor to come and clean up the mess. I envied that student.

Mr. Geisler, a grandfatherly older janitor, would come to the classroom to see the size of the job. He then shuffled off and returned with a broom, dustpan, a big trash bucket, and a smaller bucket. The small bucket held pink sawdust, the magic potion of floor cleaning. He sprinkled a good layer of the sawdust on the barf and let it settle for a minute. He then swept the mess into a dustpan and put it in the trash bucket. The whole job was done in only a few minutes, but it was welcome entertainment for all of us except for the kid who had thrown up.

Counting Down a Movie

Counting down a movie is the least of the crimes I remember from the Elmore School. It happened one day when our class was in about fourth grade. All of us grade school kids had gathered in the gym for a movie.

Movies were a special treat, and we were excited when we had them. Chairs were set up in rows on the basketball court facing a movie screen hanging above the stage. The big, gray 16-mm movie projector was pointed at the screen, and we could see from the amount of the film on the reel that this was going to be a pretty long movie. We talked together as quietly as we could, but it was hard to stay quiet.

Mr. Hetrick came in and went to the movie projector. One of the teachers turned off the gym lights. Mr. Hetrick clicked on the projector, and designs flickered on the screen. Then numbers came on the screen, counting down: "15 – 14 – 13 – 12." Someone yelled, "Eleven! Ten!" and then everybody started yelling and counting down: "Nine! Eight! Seven! Six!"

Suddenly the numbers stopped. The projector had stopped. Mr. Hetrick turned the lights on and stood in front of us kids. We knew we were in trouble.

"No more movie today!" Mr. Hetrick said. "You know you're not supposed to yell out those numbers like that. I've told you before."

Gloom fell over the gym. We just stared at the blank screen. The fun was over, and we still had two periods of school left that afternoon. We paraded back to our classrooms, too sad to talk.

I don't remember if I yelled the numbers that day, though I knew all of them. I don't even remember being told not to yell out numbers when we had movies. But I do know now, and I'll never yell out numbers if I'm seeing a movie and numbers start counting down.

Students' Entertaining Innovations

To ease the challenges or boredom at school, students were innovative. The school must have been a beehive of invention and innovation and good ideas. I can only report on a few ways some of us entertained ourselves.

During class, I often escaped in daydreams, and this surely contributed to my low standing in the class when we graduated in 1957. I was sometimes awakened from a daydream when my name, pronounced by the teacher, penetrated my wandering thoughts. I also drew pictures on the edges of my classwork papers, but I didn't claim they were artwork. They were just for me in my little school world, though my teachers had to overlook them when grading my more serious work.

Creativity really came alive at recess. When we were only in first or second grade, nearly all of us played cowboys—even the girls. I had vague ideas about cowboys, and I learned more at recess. I learned that being a cowboy could involve running and hopping in an uneven way while slapping my hips to imitate the sound of horses' hooves. Most of the kids did the same. We sounded authentic, at least to ourselves.

There arose a controversy about who was the "King of the Cowboys." One group said it was Roy Rogers. Another group supported Gene Autry. I had never been inside a movie house, and TV was just a glimmer on the horizon, so I had heard of neither of those famous cowboys. I kept quiet, and the controversy soon blew itself out.

My class may have been in fourth grade when marbles became a fad. The marbles players brought their own bags of marbles to school, and we "played marbles" at recess and lunchtime. To start a game, we laid small marbles inside a circle drawn in the dirt and took turns standing outside the circle shooting at them with our larger "shooter marbles." If we hit one of our friends' marbles, it was ours to keep if we were "playing for keeps." Otherwise, we gave back the marbles we'd won when the bell rang, and recess ended.

I don't remember any of the marbles breaking from being shot at or from being a shooter. I do remember a few marbles in which the colored glass formed colors that reminded me of beautiful sunsets. Marbles like that had hypnotic power. I could gaze at them a minute and be on an imaginary seashore.

We also played jacks at recess. That game called for a bag of the spikey little jacks and a rubber ball. You were supposed to pick up the jacks while the ball was in the air, and girls usually did this more gracefully than the boys.

I carried a pocketknife to school at most grade levels, beginning quite young. My favorite had a plastic handle with colorful, random shapes of many colors that resembled a kaleidoscope. Most boys carried knives to school, and it didn't occur to the powers that be to disarm us lest we hijack planes or overpower the school principal. None of us brought guns to school.

My pockets were usually filled with other fascinating things. The stuff in my pockets said a lot about who I was. There was hair from my dog, Lady, in the empty case of a cigarette lighter after she ran away. A medical kit in a small jar was ready for emergencies that never arose. And there was string for some unknown purpose and other things that are now too ancient to be remembered.

Heel plates on shoes were a special thrill, and we could buy them in a couple of stores in Elmore. With heel plates, we could walk down the terrazzo halls, making a musical sound with every step. Heel plates tinkled against the floor like tiny cymbals and added importance to the kids who wore them. A few girls had heel plates, and some kids even had toe plates as well.

(*Heel plates for men's and women's shoes are available now via the internet by searching "heel plates" as key words.*)

I confess that for a short time, maybe a month or two in about fourth grade, I cursed and swore during recess with help from two accomplices. One of my accomplices was a girl whose name cannot be revealed here because I have forgotten everything except her great skill at swearing. The other was a boy, also long forgotten. The girl had a vocabulary so razor sharp that it could have etched glass. I did my part, but I don't know where I got the words. Any of them would have gotten my mouth washed out with soap at home, but at school they were a triumph of dramatic expression.

I don't remember now if the curse words we used at school were mainly theological or of the biological kind. Probably our outbursts of swearing ranged across both forbidden universes. But then, in the same way that our swearing had started for no particular reason, it died out and we stopped except for occasional emergencies. No one had caught us swearing. The words simply had lost their power from overuse and had evaporated into the air around the school.

Snow Days

Snow days were one of my favorite parts of school. Northern Ohio was (and still is) subject to powerful storm fronts that come raging across Lake Erie from Canada or from the west, gaining momentum in the flat lands of Northern Illinois and Indiana. Howling blizzards could make winters exciting and travel impossible. Or the weather might become wet and cold enough to form ice on the trees and power lines, causing power failures that took people back to pre-electric times. For any of those or other reasons, one of the greatest joys of school life was *not* having school.

Weather forecasts were not good enough in the 1940s to tell people in advance if a storm would be big enough to close the school. Ice storms were especially hard to predict, so school closures for ice were usually a big surprise. Still, our favorites were snow days with actual snow.

Radio was the only way my family learned about snow days. We didn't have a telephone or a TV until I was in high school. My mother was almost always the bearer of the good news. She was up early and she listened to the radio, especially when the weather looked bad. She heard the news of the closings long before we kids were to get up for school, and she gave herself a little more peace before she told us kids. When we were young, we kids would shriek and run around the house in excitement before breakfast. After breakfast, we spent the day playing in the snow. Older kids took the news more calmly, in almost reverent thankfulness.

Snowball Fights

Our school was well-run and peaceful, but its peace was interrupted a few times by law-breaking. One of the most common forms of law-breaking was throwing snowballs. The penalty for throwing snowballs was a trip to Mr. Hetrick's office for two swift swats of the wooden paddle he kept in a closet in his office. The paddle strokes were only strong enough to emphasize the consequences of breaking the law. Boys often laughed when they got them.

When I was in about fourth grade, our entire class conspired to have a snowball fight during recess, blatantly violating the school rule. Girls joined the boys in the conspiracy. We threw snowballs at each other and were giddy in our rebellion.

Our fun was short-lived. A jealous student or a conscientious teacher turned us in, or maybe one of us threw a snowball at the wrong kid. We were all arrested and marched to the office. Mr. Hetrick reminded us of the punishment for snowballs, and he sent the girls to his conference room while we boys were instructed to wait our turn in his office.

We giggled as we heard the girls squeal (some cried) when they received their two swats. Next the boys were summoned. One by one we took our two swats. We tried to suppress our laughter so as not to mar the dignity of the moment.

That day may have been the last snowball fight for our class, but I can't swear to it.

....
Owen Drops a Chair

A memorable crime was committed by just one student, not a mob of fourth graders. The criminal in this case was my brother Owen. He was a good student, and he was well-behaved, unlike some people I could name. But in a moment of whimsy, Owen flirted briefly with crime and danger.

On a balmy lunchtime in spring 1957, Owen and some of his scholarly friends were entertaining each other in the second-floor business classroom. The classroom looked out on the large athletic field that was the recreation area for junior high and high school students. Elmore East Road ran along the south edge of the play field, and the school was visible to everyone entering town on that road. The second-floor business classroom was especially visible.

Caught up in the horseplay going on in the room, a few boys dreamed up a brilliant idea. Why not hang a chair out the window so people on the road would see it? To most of the boys the idea was only for talk, but Owen liked the idea, and the boys dared him to do it. He unwisely took the dare.

Owen's plan was to tie a window curtain cord to one of the classroom's heavy oak desk chairs. He would tie the other end of the cord to the post between two windows as an anchor. He planned to lower the chair out the window until the cord was tight, and let it hang until after lunchtime. After lunch, he would pull the chair up and bring it inside.

Things didn't work out as Owen had planned. He did tie the cord to the desk chair and the window frame, and he did carefully lower the desk chair by hand as far as he could. But the cord between window frame and the chair was too long. There was slack in the line. If he let go of the chair, the cord might snap when the chair fell and took up the slack. After a minute, his hands were tired. His fingers slipped. The chair fell. The curtain cord snapped. The chair fell and crashed into a row of shrubs between the building and a sidewalk.

Lots of people outside the school heard the crash, especially the teacher who was supervising the kids out on the field from a covered entrance next to the bushes. She was out of the path of the falling chair, but the chair landed close enough to give her a good scare. (If the chair had hit anyone, it would have been a catastrophe.)

Owen got more attention than he wanted. Word spread fast. Teachers, coaches, and kids came running to the scene of the crime. Some looked up at the window, and for a few minutes Owen was there, looking down at the fallen chair.

Mr. Herbert Katko, one of the coaches, appeared at the scene. He looked at the chair and the open window and then rushed into the building to arrest the perpetrator. Kids who had been in the room fingered Owen for the angry investigator. After putting together the sketchy facts, Mr. Katko announced throughout the halls that a student had tried to kill a teacher by dropping a chair on her. He summarily marched Owen off to see Mr. Hetrick.

Mr. Hetrick had a calmer, more judicial temperament. Owen was a good student with a spotless record, so he got off with a light sentence, if any. I thought he might have been suspended from school for a week and might have had to apologize to the teacher he had frightened. To this day, he still refuses to admit he suffered any serious consequences.

(The story is worth telling because it's such a departure from Owen's usual nature. He graduated from Elmore High School third in his class, and he graduated from college with high honors. For forty years he was a computer engineer at NASA. The chair incident was not an early experiment in space flight.)

....

Elvis Invades Elmore

No account of school life in the 1950s would be complete without Elvis. He sang and wiggled and seduced some of us, and no one escaped his impact.

Elvis may never have been in Elmore, at least not physically. His driver may never have taken him up the town hill and past Rader's Dime Store and Damschroder's Dry Goods Store. He may never have been driven through town on his way from Toledo to some other great cultural center, and he sure didn't put on a show at our high school. Elvis was too busy to spend time in Elmore. He was dazzling youthful mobs across the country, making girls scream and cry in their first exposure to his magnetic presence.

But Elvis did invade Elmore.

The first thunderbolt from the Elvis firmament came soon after his first big song hit the airwaves. "Heartbreak Hotel" was released on January 27, 1956, and broke into homes all the way from Elmore to Leatherport and beyond. The effect was electric. Young kids like me didn't stop to analyze why we were so drawn to his music. It was just *there*, right on the radio, and it called us to worship in rapt attention. Elvis sounded faintly like some other singers, but he was a different experience. My own timidly rebellious genes quickened to the sound of his songs. I was sixteen.

Leatherport, Ohio

One Saturday afternoon in late winter 1956 I was upstairs in our home on Graytown Road. I turned on the large heterodyne radio. Its tubes warmed and glowed and brought in CKLW from across Lake Erie in Windsor, Canada. Elvis was on all afternoon. I puttered at some forgotten project that afternoon, and I was overcome by the throbbing, wailing, wooing, crooning music. That afternoon was a conversion experience; I joined the youth cult of 1956, long before "youth cult" was part of our vocabulary.

On Monday morning, I boarded the school bus with my siblings as usual, but now I was a changed man, or a changed boy of sixteen. I had heard the siren call of a world far beyond Leatherport and Elmore. On the school bus Elvis was going through my mind. The farm fields suddenly seemed more distant. I was suddenly a foreigner to those familiar scenes of hogs, cows, and corn. School was like something seen in a dream that day and for many days after.

Jim Derickson rode the same bus, and from then until we graduated, we rehearsed Elvis songs on the bus. We both had our favorite Elvis moments, but Jim was much more convincing. He even had a longer, oiled-down ducktail hairstyle that I couldn't imitate. He could snap his fingers and sing, and he seemed more convincing and more seductive than I was. As high school juniors we were older than nearly all the other kids on the bus, so they tolerated us, even if some wanted to mock and scoff.

Our junior year rolled on through the spring, and in September 1956 our class became the Senior Class of 1957. Elvis had followed me right into my senior year. He had invaded my mind and emotions, even if he hadn't physically conquered Elmore.

An electrifying announcement burst into my little world: Elvis is coming! I must have heard the messianic news on the radio. Elvis would perform at the Toledo Sports Arena on Thanksgiving Day, November 22, 1956. How I emerged from my larval isolation and found a way to buy a ticket, I don't know. The price may have been $5, or maybe even $10. Either would have been a princely sum when I earned $1 an hour for farm work. When the great evening arrived, I had my precious ticket to see "Elvis in Concert."

My parents and siblings must have looked on in fear for my body and soul as I combed my hair and fastened the top button on my flannel shirt. No one tried to dissuade me from my worldly mission that night; it would have been useless. I had heard the call and responded.

The nerd who saw Elvis in Toledo on November 22, 1956 as he looked then.

I drove my parents' maroon, white-top 1952 Buick LeSabre. I would have driven a sleek, powerful sports car, but we didn't have a sleek, powerful sports car, only a 1952 Buick sedan. Leaving early, I pulled onto Graytown Road and headed north toward the shimmering lights of Toledo. How I found my way to the Sport Arena fifty years before Google Maps, I don't know, maybe by a migratory instinct.

Inside the Sports Arena, I found my reserved seat about three-fourths of the way back from the stage on one side of the oval building. My seat was on bleachers four feet above the hockey rink, and there were hundreds of seats on the rink itself. I was high enough to see over those on the floor. The stage was in clear view but far away.

When I arrived, I was nearly alone in my section of the bleachers. Soon other Elvis fans came, and they looked like real Elvis followers. They seemed to be a few years older; their hair was oiled and combed into beautiful ducktails. Their black leather jackets sparkled with silver studs, and most of the boys wore harness boots. The girls wore leather pants and leather jackets, and their makeup was worldlier than any I had seen in church or at Harris-Elmore High School. Many of my fellow Elvis fans were smoking cigarettes, and a cloud of smoke hovered over the Sports Arena. I didn't look directly at my fellow Elvis fans. I did not want to attract their attention in any way.

The young men seemed to have the girls under their control. The men never screamed or applauded; they scowled all the time, a clear sign of coolness. If the girls wanted to scream, they didn't show it. I didn't scream, either.

The program was scheduled to last from 7:00 until 10:00. I naively expected Elvis to sing for a solid three hours. Maybe he would sing some of my favorites more than once, and I was fine with that. Just before 7:00, the lights dimmed and spotlights played on the stage through clouds of cigarette smoke. A man in a flashy suit strode onto the stage and grasped a microphone. He greeted us warmly and promised us a great evening of entertainment. But then he said, "Now for our first act of the night, here are the Blissful Crooners," or something like that. They sang a few bland 1950s songs, and I waited for Elvis.

The flashy man came back and announced another singing group. One after another, Southern Gospel or other country-sounding groups sang. They were rewarded with silence and indifference. If there were a few kids who politely clapped their hands, I don't remember. I was busy ignoring the warm-up acts. I just wanted to see Elvis.

When my senses and my seat were numbed from the parade of musical groups, there was a "pregnant pause." The stage was empty. The smart money in the Sports Arena knew this silence meant the real show was about to begin. A murmur swept across the crowd and rose nearly to a roar. A man took center stage. Behind him a male quartet took a position near the back of the stage beside a man at a piano and two men with guitars. The smart money knew these were The Jordanaires, Elvis's backup harmony team. Crowd noise rose like the wind before a summer storm.

"Now you will hear the man you came to hear," the announcer yelled. "Here he is! *Elvis Presley!*"

Elvis Himself burst onto the stage. Screaming and applause were deafening. Elvis strode across the stage from side to side, waving and bowing. He greeted the policemen who were there to preserve his life from his adoring fans. Elvis Himself took mighty steps to center stage, and pressed his famous lips to the microphone. All was silent. Elvis Himself then said, "Woof!"

More screams from the crowd. Elvis took the microphone again and sang, "Well since my baby left me, I've found a new place to dwell, it's down at the end of Lonely Street, it's Heartbreak Hotel!" The crowd noise nearly drowned out the King of Rock 'n' Roll.

"Heartbreak Hotel" led to other Elvis songs that were already hits or soon would be. A jazzed-up Elvis version of a Pat Boone song was next. When he sang "Hound Dog," Elvis Himself crouched at the edge of the stage and pointed in the face of a policeman: "You ain't nothin' but a hound dog, cryin' all the time! You ain't never caught a rabbit and you ain't no friend of mine!" We devoted fans howled laughing.

Elvis Himself sang for about half an hour. His last song might have been "Love Me Tender," one he had released a week earlier. Then Elvis Himself disappeared. We waited for him to reappear and accept our worshipful applause. He didn't come back.

A man came to the stage. It may have been Colonel Parker, Elvis' promoter. In a somber voice of finality, he announced, "Elvis has left the building! He's gone!"

Hysterical screaming broke out. Somewhere down on the hockey rink girls were sobbing, pulling their hair, and tearing their clothing. Boys were standing stunned. The cool guys in the leather jackets near me lit new cigarettes, took their girls' arms, and stood to leave. I got up and got out of their way, but I didn't light a cigarette. I just wanted to mind my own business, find my car, and get back to Leatherport.

I eased my beautiful Buick through the parking lot traffic until the car and I were free to head down Woodville Road to Route 163. It had been an experience of a lifetime. And I was glad to have lived through it.

(When I went to college in 1957 I was still an Elvis fan. I bought a 33 1/3 album of Elvis songs that year. Sometime that year, Jailhouse Rock *came to a movie theater for a midnight show in downtown Anderson, Indiana, where I was in college. I walked alone to the theater and found myself surrounded by hundreds of fans who looked like my compatriots at the Sport Arena concert in Toledo. I again thought it best not to be too curious about my fellow Elvis fans. The atmosphere was not as electric as it had been at the Sport Arena when Elvis Himself was there with us. The movie crowd was sullen rather than hysterical. The movie's story line may have tainted the movie. That night may have been when I began to outgrow Elvis. Within a year, Elvis was ruling the musical world, but I had wandered away to other things and other music. I'm glad I went to the Sports Arena in Toledo that night, and I'm glad I didn't go again.*

Elvis's show at Toledo was on November 22, 1956. Seven years later, November 22, 1963, became a date that lives in infamy.)

Classmates for Life

On Memorial Day weekend in 1957, when the Class of 1957 was about to graduate, we couldn't have guessed that we would be as attached to each other as we have become in these later years. On that graduation night, we'd all had enough of each other and were just excited to be graduating and getting out of school, maybe forever.

Some classmates went off into the night with their diplomas, never to be seen again. Some would return to Elmore only for quick, unannounced visits. Others returned for just a few of the annual alumni banquets at the school. Some came frequently, even from far away. Some settled near enough to remain in contact with each other. Some live right in Elmore within walking distance of the school.

The first to die was Alice Avers, who died in childbirth in 1963. Robert Waterman was the next early death. Our numbers will dwindle more in the coming years.

As our years on earth piled up, most members of the Class of '57 found new appreciation for the experiences we shared in the Harris-Elmore School. We began to attend the Alumni Banquet on Memorial Day weekend, and we started staging our own class reunions, clinging to friendships and memories that we value more highly as time passes.

We remain classmates for life, whether we will see each other again here on earth or must await that one greatest of all reunions in heaven. On that other shore, we will have crossed a barrier even greater than the Portage River that flows through Elmore and past the hidden ruins of historic Leatherport, Ohio.

The class of 1957 just starting out in 1945.

Acknowledgments

I'M GRATEFUL TO Karen Roberts for her expert editing, and she's not to be blamed for lack of clarity that may remain. Katie Blum, the research librarian at the Elmore Library found amazing details again and again. I'm grateful to Katie for her skillful research and to the Elmore Library for having such interest in local history. Heather Carter's maps of Leatherport and Elmore are beautifully drawn and aid the reader's understanding of those locations. Heather also proofed the book. Spenser Benefield provided most of the photos and has entered them into the Elmore Library's archives. Doug Pickard and Nancy Pries researched the names of all students who were members of the Class of 1957 in our twelve years of schooling. Jack Haar read a late version of the book and made helpful comments. John Votaw, an Elmore classmate, tried to save me from myself when he read the manuscript. Larry Kardatzke read the book did a meticulous job of copy editing that would do credit to a professional. Copy editing, layout, and the book's design are the work of the staff at 1106 Design.

Appendix A: Other Sources

THE MOST AUTHORITATIVE BOOK on the history of Elmore is Grace Luebke's *Elmore, Ohio, a History Preserved*, 1975, Revised in 1998. The book was printed by Windmill Publications, 6628 Uebelhack Road, Mount Vernon, Indiana 47620. Grace Luebke was the director of the Harris–Elmore Public Library for over thirty years. She developed the local history section of the library during her working years and in retirement.

Detailed stories about early Elmore appear in *Elmore's One Hundred Years 1851 to 1951* by Newell Witte, a journalist and photographer who spent his life in the area of the Black Swamp after it was drained, populated, and made into one of the greatest farming and industrial areas in the United States. In his booklet, he reports that Joseph Harris arrived at the site of Elmore in 1818 to trade with the Ottawa Indians, and Harris Township was named for him. Also, in the summer of 1823, Ezekiel Rice and his brother Reuben came from near Columbus and became among the first residents of Elmore, not realizing that Rice Street in Elmore would be named for them. The short, 60-page book is not available on Amazon, but it is available in the Elmore, Ohio, library.

The Toledo, Port Clinton and Lakeside Railway, Montevallo Historical Press (June 1, 1997) by George W. Hilton is a detailed history of the construction and operation of the interurban train line.

Elmore Public Library, Grace Luebke Local History Center

The public library in Elmore, Ohio, is a treasure to Elmorites near and far. A visit to the library can take you to places you might only read about. Besides books, there are movies, recordings, and story times. The Grace Luebke Local History Center contains a wealth of information online and for in-person inspection. A research assistant provides online assistance about people, places and events.

Ottawa County Historical Society

A wealth of information about Ottawa County history is available online from the Ottawa County Historical Society at https://ottawacounty history.org/

Ottawa County Genealogical Society

County history and genealogical results are available online at the society's website: http://www.ocogs.org/

Appendix B: Elmore's 1951 Businesses

Elmore Businesses

These businesses paid for ads in Newell Witte's 1951 centennial book.

A.J. Weis Grocery

Almroth Block Company:
   Robert, William, and Clarence
   Almroth

Bank of Elmore, Ralph Magee,
   President

Brandes and Trautman Frozen
   Food Lockers

Brandes and Trautman Wholesale
   Meats, George Brandes and
   Loren Trautman

Carl Haar Building and
   Remodeling

Damschroder's Service, Lincoln
   Damschroder

Damschroder's Store

Dolph Oil Company, James Dolph

Dunmyer Dairy, Lindsey

Elmore Cleaners, Ronald Kruse

Elmore Hardware, William
   Kontak

Elmore Lumber and Builder's Supply, Stanley Slates

Elmore Manufacturing, Calvin Magsig

Elmore Tribune

George W. Brandow Agency

Harry Redman Service Station, Toledo and Rice Streets

Hovis Grocery, John Hovis

Jaeger Hardware

Johnnie's Electric Service

Kuhlman Service, Harold Kuhlman

Laurie Dolph Service Station

Max Reynolds Plumbing and Heating

Multiplex Machinery Corporation

Neeb Motor Sales

Norwalk Truck Line (John Ernsthausen)

Ottawa Basket Factory, Harry Deacon

Paul Haar – Hay, Straw, and Grain

Pickard Greenhouse

Portage Inn, Marvin Lohr

Riverside Dairy, Woodville

Sabroske and Myers, Fred Sabroske and Richard Myers

Snac Bar, Charles Longenecker

Tank's Meats

The Famers' Elevator Company

Toledo Edison Company, Thomas Edison

Truman Drug

Walter J. Avers, Rawleigh Good Health Products

Walter Linker Insurance

Waters Insurance Agency, D.G. Waters

Wehners Barber Shop, Don Wehner

Weis Brothers Coal and Builders Supply, George and Frank Weis

Wel-Com-In Restaurant, Alvin Doepker

Williston Implement Company, Williston

Woodraft Contractor and Builder, L.R. Henry

Yeagle Decorating Service, Carlton Yeagle

Appendix C: Elmore Graduating Class of 1957

These are the names of the graduating class members as we knew them in school. The married names of the girls are in parentheses.

1. Alice Avers (Heckman)
2. Jim Bolander
3. Trinidad Cuevas (Jaramillo)
4. Linden Damschroder
5. Larry Deacon
6. Jane Deitemyer
7. Jim Derickson
8. Tom Dolph
9. Carol Fondesy (Schanke)
10. Shirley Giffin (Damschroder)
11. Carol Guth (Foss)
12. Nancy Haar (Pries)
13. Beatrice Hetrick (Neuman)
14. Karen Hetrick (Johns)
15. Karen Jacobs
16. Patti James (Smith)
17. Milan Kardatzke
18. Miles Kardatzke

19. Nyle Kardatzke

20. Lowell Knierem

21. Janet Kuhlman (Gregory)

22. Bill Kuhlman

23. Bob Kuhlman

24. Ruth Ann Longnecker (Traver)

25. Barbara Magsig (Rollins)

26. Barbara Moellman

27. John Morris

28. Marilyn Nissen (Klickman)

29. Rex Ohl

30. Judy Owen

31. Doug Pickard

32. Faye Rothert (Rhiel)

33. Shirley Sahr (Lemke)

34. Lyle Schlievert

35. Lynda Semrock (Bauman)

36. Lisa Sparkes (Spera)

37. John Votaw

38. Bob Waterman

39. Bud Widmer

40. Jo Ann Widmer

41. Alan Witt

42. Danny Wood

Appendix D: All Members of the Class of 1957 from 1945 to 1957

Thanks to research by Doug Pickard and Nancy Pries, these are the kids who were in the Class of 1957 during our years at Elmore. Our stable farming community saw much change before forty-two of us graduated together in 1957.

1. Avers, Alice
2. Barkhau, Catherine
3. Below, Marge
4. Below, R.
5. Bolander, Jim
6. Buhrow, Willard
7. Chasteen, Marvin
8. Chio, Joanne
9. Cuevas, Pedro
10. Cuevas, Trinidad
11. Damschroder, Linden
12. Deacon, Larry
13. Deitemyer, Jane
14. Derickson, Jim

15. Dolph, Tom
16. Duran, Mary
17. Durdel, Roger
18. Fondessy, Carol
19. Frania, Joanne
20. Geldeen, Earl
21. Goetz, Vernell
22. Griffin, Shirley
23. Guth, Carol
24. Haar, Nancy
25. Harder, James
26. Heineman, Mary Ann
27. Henry, Nelson
28. Hesselbart, Sandra
29. Hetrick, Beatrice
30. Hetrick, Karen
31. Jacobs, Karen
32. James, Patti
33. Johnson, Alice
34. Kardatzke, Milan
35. Kardatzke, Miles
36. Kardatzke, Nyle
37. Knieriem, Lowell
38. Kuhlman, Bill
39. Kuhlman, Bob
40. Kuhlman, Janet
41. Lauer, Donald
42. Lemke, Alice
43. Longnecker, Ruth Ann
44. Magsig, Barbara
45. Malone, Patricia
46. Moellman, Barbara
47. Moore, Patsy
48. Morris, John
49. Nissen, Marilyn
50. Nuhfer, Patty
51. Ohl, Rex
52. Orman, Gaylord
53. Orman, Wilbur
54. Ory, Dennis
55. Overmyer, David
56. Overmyer (unknown)
57. Owen, Judy
58. Peters, Mary Lou
59. Pickard, Doug
60. Plumlee, Charles
61. Renwand, Gary
62. Reynolds, Mary Lou

Appendix D: All Members of the Class of 1957 from 1945 to 1957

63. Roberts, D.

64. Rochester, Lester

65. Rodriguez, Julia

66. Roepke, Dave

67. Rothert, Faye

68. Ruckman, Doris

69. Sahr, Shirley

70. Sarnes, Wilma

71. Schlievert, Lyle

72. Semrock, Lynda

73. Shimp, Jim

74. Sondergeld, Raymond

75. Sparkes, Lisa

76. Suhrbier, Lee

77. Votaw, John

78. Waterman, Robert

79. Wheatly, Twyla

80. Widmer, Jo Ann

81. Widmer, Bud

82. Witt, Alan

83. Wood, Danny

84. Zilles, Eddie